A Teacher's Reflection Book

A Teacher's Reflection Book

Exercises, Stories, Invitations

Jean Koh Peters

Mark Weisberg

Foreword by
Gerry Hess
Co-Director, Institute for
Law Teaching and Learning

CAROLINA ACADEMIC PRESS
Durham, North Carolina

Copyright © 2011
Carolina Academic Press
All Rights Reserved

Library of Congress Cataloging-in-Publication Data

Peters, Jean Koh, 1958-
A teacher's reflection book : exercises, stories, invitations / Jean
Koh Peters and Mark Weisberg.
p. cm.
Includes bibliographical references and index.
ISBN 978-1-59460-942-8 (alk. paper)
1. Teaching--Methodology. 2. Teachers--Training of I. Weis-
berg, Mark II. Title.

LB1025.3.P466 2011
371.1--dc23

2011016487

CAROLINA ACADEMIC PRESS
700 Kent Street
Durham, North Carolina 27701
Telephone (919) 489-7486
Fax (919) 493-5668
www.cap-press.com

Printed in the United States of America.

For Susan, and in memory of Donald L. Finkel
For Jim, Liz, and Chris
For our students

Contents

Foreword	xi
Preface	xiii
Gratitudes	xxiii
Chapter 1 • How Does a Teacher Say Hello?	3
I. A Look at Several First Classes	8
II. Exercises to Focus on Hello	13
A. What Is the First Experience Students Have in Your Course? What Is Their First Experience in Class?	14
B. What Are the Dispositions of Your Classroom?	15
C. Fast Forward Through the Semester You're about to Start	16
D. Consider "Entrainment" and the Rhythms of Your Semester	17
E. Think about Hellos in Popular Culture	17
F. How Will You Deal with Fluctuating Student Attendance During "Shopping Periods"?	18
G. What Will Be the Role of Technology in Your Classroom, and Will You Make Space to Express That in Your Hello?	18
H. Will You Know Your Students' Names?	18
I. How Will You Handle Your Announcements?	19
J. As You Begin, How Do You Want the Central Ideas of the Course to Emerge?	19
K. Consider Generating Ideas by Using Beginning Rituals in Other Settings	20
III. Final Thoughts about Hello	20
IV. Conclusion	23
Notes	24

vii

Chapter 2 • Reflection: What It Is and How to Practice It   25

  I. Introduction: A Reflection on the Need for Reflection   25

  II. Essential Elements of Reflection — What Makes
    Reflection Work for You?   28

    A. Identify Meaningful Elements of Reflection
      That Uniquely Suit Your Needs   29

    B. Three Recommended Elements of Reflection:
      Starting Focal Point, Experience, Non-judgment   31

      1. A Starting Focal Point   32

      2. Experience   32

      3. Non-judgment   33

  III. A Session of Reflection: The Individual
    Reflection Event   39

    A. Individual Reflection Event: The Retreat Model   39

    B. Examples of Individual Reflection Events   44

      1. Reflection Event — With a Group, at
        Our Retreat   44

      2. Reflection Event — Alone, at a Conference,
        Further Reflected Upon Alone, after the
        Conference   50

  IV. What a Practice of Mindful Reflection Might Look Like   52

    A. The Spirit of Mindful Reflection — A Practice,
      Not a Habit   52

    B. The Structure of Mindful Reflection —
      Useful Strategies   55

    C. Additional Suggestions for Developing a
      Reflection Practice   56

      1. Downshifting, Making the Transition   56

      2. Giving Oneself Permission   57

      3. Dealing with Technology and Time   57

    D. Creating Conditions for Reflection   57

  V. Conclusion   59

    Notes   60

Chapter 3 • Experiments in Listening   63

  I. Looking Retrospectively at Your Experiences
    of Listening   67

CONTENTS ix

A.	Ask Analytical or General Questions about Your Listening	68
	1. Ten Freewriting/Brainstorming Prompts	68
	2. Explore Your Listening on a Doubting and Believing Spectrum	70
B.	Explore Critical Incidents from the Past	72
	1. High Points and Low Points as a Listener	72
	2. Profile of the Three Best Listeners I Know	73
	3. High Points and Low Points as a Person Being Listened To	73

II. Looking Prospectively: Analyzing Your Listening for New Insights ... 74

A. Collect New Data ... 74

B. Experiment with Your Listening ... 76

    1. Use the Doubting-Believing Spectrum: Two Variants ... 76

    2. Wait Five Seconds before Responding ... 81

    3. Don't Offer Advice ... 86

    4. Listen with Your Hands Occupied ... 86

    5. Practice Non-judgment ... 87

    6. Try a Group Exercise ... 88

Notes ... 92

Chapter 4 • Who Are Our Students, and How and What Do They Learn in Our Classrooms? ... 95

I. Who Were We as Students: Our Best/Worst Moments as Students ... 95

II. Student Voices ... 96

III. A Culture of Fear and Its Consequences ... 109

    A. Three Classrooms, Three Nightmare Scenarios ... 109

IV. What Can We Do to Facilitate Learning? ... 123

    A. Teach Non-judgmentally/Teach Non-judgment ... 123

    B. Discern the Gift, Not the Gifted ... 125

    C. Use Midstream, or Formative, Assessment ... 125

    D. Anticipate Difficult Incidents ... 127

    E. Take One More Minute ... 128

    F. Trust Ourselves ... 129

| V. Conclusion | 129 |
| Notes | 131 |

Chapter 5 • The Teacher and Vocation | **133** |
I. Discovering Vocation	135
A. Understanding Vocation	135
B. Finding Your Vocation: Four Exercises	138
1. Write Your Obituary	138
2. Find and Explore a Governing Metaphor	140
3. Compose a Job Description	141
4. Visit or Write Your Future Self	143
C. A Life Lived in Vocation: Implications	144
II. Nurturing Vocation in Ordinary Times: Two Sets of Processes You Can Trust	147
A. Internal Processes You Can Trust	149
B. External Processes You Can Trust	153
III. Some Elements of a Teacher's Vocation	155
A. Writing	156
B. Classroom Teaching	164
IV. Conclusion	166
Notes	168

Chapter 6 • How Does a Teacher Say Goodbye? | **171** |
I. Introduction	171
II. Invitations for Thinking about Goodbye	174
III. Ideas for Last Classes/Meetings	176
A. A Closing Circle	176
B. Completing the Circle	176
C. Jean's Goodbye and Coupon	177
D. Postcards and Silent Witness	178
IV. Goodbye: A Unique Moment of Reflection	180
V. Conclusion	185
Notes	187

Appendix • Resources for Reflecting | **189** |

About the Authors | **191** |

Index | **193** |

Foreword

Why do we teach? Who are our students? What can we do to help our students persevere, survive, excel? How can we continue to develop our professional and personal selves? Where will we find the time and space to address these, and many other questions, relevant to our personal and professional growth? These issues matter to thoughtful teachers at every level—elementary school physical education teachers (like my brother), high school special education teachers (like my son), social work professors (like my spouse), and law school profs (like me).

Jean Koh Peters and Mark Weisberg offer us a wonderful resource—*A Teacher's Reflection Book*—to facilitate our journey of discovery and renewal. Mark and Jean are teachers' teachers. Not because they are model teachers, colleagues, parents, or partners. Like most of us, Jean and Mark have struggled to become effective teachers and to integrate their professional and personal lives. They are teachers' teachers because they have thought deeply about how to facilitate teachers' development through reflection. They have meticulously planned and then led wildly successful reflection retreats for teachers. And now they have written this book to bring the power and magic of reflection to anyone willing to spend a bit of time reading, thinking, and writing about their teaching.

In their retreats and in this book, Mark and Jean guide teachers through the reflection process. They offer a wide variety of exercises and opportunities for us to delve more deeply into our teaching and our students' learning. Jean and Mark do not talk at us, instead they provide space and support for our reflection.

While reviewing a draft of *A Teacher's Reflection Book*, I had two experiences that illustrate the power of Mark's and Jean's work. As

xii FOREWORD

I reviewed the first half of the book, I was harried and overwhelmed with end-of-the-semester teaching, exam preparation, and grading. Reading this book was another item on an already too long To Do list. But as I began making my way though the book, I stopped often to engage in the reflection exercises Jean and Mark offered. The review became a joy rather than a chore.

While reviewing the second half of *A Teacher's Reflection Book*, I was stuck for fourteen hours in the San Francisco airport. Inspired by Mark and Jean, I spent a couple of hours engaged in a mini retreat, which they call an individual reflection event. My mini retreat helped me make the transition from semester break to a new semester. By the time I got on my long-delayed flight, I was filled with energy and ideas for my upcoming semester of teaching and scholarship. What a gift.

I hope that *A Teacher's Reflection Book* helps you embark on a valuable journey of reflection. I am confident that you are in good hands.

Gerry Hess
Professor, and Director of the
Institute for Law School Teaching
Gonzaga University School of Law

Preface

The 'secrets' of good teaching are the same as the secrets of good living: seeing oneself without blinking, offering hospitality to the alien other, speaking truth to power, being present and being real.

—Parker Palmer, Foreword to Mary Rose O'Reilley, Radical Presence[1]

Welcome to *A Teacher's Reflection Book*. Its story began eleven years ago in a beautiful room with a stone fireplace, oriental carpets, and huge windows with a view of the Cascade Mountains.[2] Gathered there were 30 law teachers from across North America who'd come to spend three days reflecting on their teaching. Some were disillusioned and had come wondering whether teaching really was their vocation. Others, while excited about their teaching, had found their academic lives so full that they welcomed an opportunity to slow their pace and enter a quiet space to reflect on what they'd been doing. Still others had come simply to rest: to walk, to swim, to read, to decompress.

Jean Koh Peters was in this last group. Exhausted from a year of teaching and difficult clinical work representing children and people seeking asylum in the United States, she had arrived a day early, with forty pounds of novels, gardening, and craft books she had been wanting to read, as well as her guitar and flute, firmly resolved not to become involved in the retreat, defended against any kind of group experience. She wanted time to herself to recover from the year.

Jean never did pick up any of those books; they went back to Connecticut unread. Instead, after talking and enjoying a wonderful meal that first day with retreat facilitator Mark Weisberg,

xiii

and walking with several participants the next day before the retreat began, she found herself drawn to the opening session, even accepting Mark's invitation to greet the entering participants with music from her flute. As the first session began, she felt herself invited into a safe, welcoming, open space, and from that moment she was fully engaged and left the retreat feeling reinvigorated and more grounded in her vocation. For almost all participants the evaluations told a similar story.

How did that happen? The participants certainly were crucial. Everyone seemed to want to spend several days connected to, or reconnecting with, their authentic selves, and most embraced the opportunity to engage with and be supported by like-minded peers. And the setting, along with the structure of the retreat, seemed to give them permission to do just that. Exercises, stories, readings, large and small group discussions, along with considerable free time for thinking, walking, writing, and talking, each in its own way conducive to reflecting.

Whatever the reasons, Gerry Hess, Director of the Institute for Law School Teaching, decided the Institute should sponsor a second retreat, and this time invited both Jean and Mark to facilitate. Mark was delighted at the prospect of working with Jean. When invited by Gerry to facilitate the initial retreat, he had been intrigued by the challenge of designing an event foregrounding reflection. As part of his planning process, he found himself returning to his favorite books about teaching and learning, parts of which found their way into the retreat materials. During the retreat, he was excited to see readings that had touched him helping to open a space for others. While fully engaged in the retreat, his role as sole facilitator left him less time than he would have liked for his own reflections. He expected that sharing the role with Jean would change that. It did, and much more. Gerry's invitation began a collaboration that has been a vital part of our working and our personal lives for the past eleven years.

Although when we agreed to work together, the retreat was three years away, we began planning almost immediately, communicating through e-mail and more significantly, in weekly, hour-long telephone conversations. We retained most of the ele-

PREFACE   xv

ments of the first retreat, adding a structured opportunity for participants to work on an "Individual Reflection Event," designed to meet their most pressing needs for reflection and feedback.[3] We also added an arts space and sang rounds. This retreat was equally well-received, and it was clear that the additions contributed to its success.

For the most recent retreat, in July 2005,[4] we expanded its audience, opening it to all university teachers. We were apprehensive about whether people from diverse disciplines—the list included Business, Law, Exercise and Sports Science, French, Asian Studies, Education, Drama, English, and Psychology—would be able to work meaningfully across those disciplines and support each other, but we needn't have worried.

Through it all we wondered why the insights that emerged from this experience, and the experience itself, had to be reserved for three days in a wonderful setting with perfect weather, delicious food, and comfortable accommodations. Why couldn't we try to make them available to a larger audience? When Gerry suggested we should do just that, we decided to give it a go. This book is the result.

At first we were daunted by the idea of trying to recreate in black and white what had felt so linked to a specific time and place. We came to realize, however, that our goal was not to recreate the retreats, but to serve the same purpose the retreats served: to help dedicated teachers who were committed to reflection, but who simply couldn't figure out how to work it into their daily lives, to find that time and structure that reflection. Our goal at our retreats has been to help teachers begin to craft a daily life of reflection that could be continued in the hurly-burly of work back home. The mini-retreat we've called the Individual Reflection Event (see Chapter 2) was designed, both to allow participants to have that mini-retreat while attending the retreat, but also, by learning that they could design one and by participating in others their colleagues had designed, to encourage them to create similar mini-retreats for themselves, which they could work into their daily lives at home.

We have designed this book so that you can use its materials as part of those reflection events, those mini-retreats, either on your own, with a friend or colleague, or with a group of colleagues over time. Just as our retreat participants went home with huge, heavy three-ring binders filled with some of our favorite writings about teaching and learning and our favorite exercises for prompting reflection, we hope that you'll find this book a companion, inviting you to reflection, supporting you through the difficult times that sometimes can accompany our teaching.

Some writers refer to retreats as time in "sacred space."[5] Using that definition, it's easy to understand why busy teachers want time to retreat; in normal academic life, reflection feels impossible. What is sacred about faculty meetings, PowerPoint presentations, exam booklets, and grading? Yet, when we have been able to gather with other teachers to talk about teaching, inevitably we have found that our teaching contains a meaning and heart so important to us that the chance to reflect on it seriously feels not a burden, but a joy. We also discovered that many of our participants already had found a variety of ways to reflect on their teaching but hadn't identified them or figured out how to regularize them. And we learned that no matter how many ways they might have to reflect on their teaching, people welcome more.

We hope you might find this book useful in those precious moments of reflecting on the teaching work we are privileged to do. As our section on the individual reflection event suggests, we believe that the four essential elements of retreating—preparing an intention to explore, entering into a contained time or space, listening mindfully, and reemerging transformed into ordinary time and space—can become part of even the most harried professional teaching life. We hope this book will be a companion for you as you move in and out of your work life and your reflection time and will help provide a link between the two, so that reflection becomes a necessary and regular part of your already rich lives.

And you needn't reflect alone. One of our greatest pleasures in facilitating these retreats has been to meet other teachers who share our desire to reflect. The company of good colleagues is a joy unrivaled, and we encourage you to explore whether you might use this book in conversation with other like-minded teachers. But because so many of our readings are by teachers, for teachers, even

PREFACE   xvii

if you are working on your own, using these materials will help you to enter many conversations with fine teachers of all stripes.

Consequently, as we've done in our retreats, we invite you to join us and enter what we hope will be a safe, supportive space in which you can find your unique path for reflecting on your teaching, alone, and possibly with others.

To help you on that path, we've included a variety of prompts for reflecting. Throughout the book you'll find exercises that, following Don Finkel, author of the provocative *Teaching with Your Mouth Shut*,* we hope you'll feel encouraged to try rather than just read. Some of the exercises you can do either alone or with a group. We also ask questions and occasionally offer our responses to them. We include stories, our own and those of others. And in each section we include a set of what we hope will be provocative readings, not an exhaustive survey of a topic, but a selection of favorites.

Some of the exercises and readings will appeal to you more than others. We don't expect you to respond to each. Rather, we've tried to provide enough variety that each of you will be able to craft your own reflective journey through the book. We intend the book to be exploratory, not hortatory. And while it has a structure and we do have our perspectives, we haven't constructed the book as an argument. Rather, to echo Mary Rose O'Reilley:

> [Our] method is more circling than linear. This book is not a how-to manual, still less an argument developed from premise to conclusion. It is a collection of exercises, stories, tropes, and images that nudge up against each other and try to reproduce the "analysis" as an experience,

---

  * "It's almost impossible to get people to put their book down and perform some task while they are reading. Nevertheless, I shall attempt the impossible. I would like you to stop reading this book long enough to take this simple test …

Find a piece of paper. Put from your mind what you have read in this book so far. Answer the following question in writing …"
Donald L. Finkel, *Teaching with Your Mouth Shut* (Portsmouth, NH: Boynton/ Cook, 2000).

an experience [we] hope [you] will share the living-of. Instead of constructing an argument in theoretical terms, [we're] trying to "make it happen" …[6]

You can approach the book from several perspectives. You can use it to explore personal dimensions in your life, or you can use it to explore professional dimensions. As the opening quote from Parker Palmer suggests, for us these are intimately linked, and we invite you to explore whether that's true for you. However you approach it, remember that a retreat is meant for an audience of one. So as you proceed, we encourage you to trust your own process and to use whatever methods work for you.

How the Book Is Organized

The book contains six chapters, each divided into sections. Chapter 1 begins, unsurprisingly, at the beginning, with *Saying Hello.* Teachers say many hellos, and they aren't always easy. As teachers, we want to make our first encounters meaningful, to be both inviting and engaging, possibly even provocative. In this section, we say hello to you and explore what is significant about saying hello and how we might do it. We offer you a variety of exercises and introduce you to several thoughtful teachers reflecting on their teaching. Perhaps as you engage their voices, you'll want to begin to add your own.

If you were to describe ***your*** *ideal teacher, what qualities would she have? What relationship would she establish with you?*

In Chapter 2 we focus explicitly on reflection: what it is and how to practice it meaningfully. We invite you to think about the teacher you are or try to be. Exploring the value of reflecting, we identify critical elements in any reflective process, offer a model for using that process, which allows you personalize it by helping you locate what we call "processes you can trust."

An extremely useful method for employing these processes can be an *individual reflection event,* an opportunity to listen to yourself, and possibly to others, on an issue or concern important to you. At the past two retreats, we invited each person to identify

PREFACE

that issue for themselves and provided a structure that would ensure them the time for deep reflection on their issue and for others to support them in whatever ways they wished. We've tried to do that again here, providing several examples of successful individual reflection events.

When we reflect, we create a space where we can listen to ourselves, and in a supportive group, to others, including our students. Listening not only is essential for reflection; much of our lives consists of listening and being listened to. We've devoted Chapter 3 to exploring how we listen and what that might mean for us and for our interlocutors.

It's impossible to reflect meaningfully on our teaching without thinking about our students: who they are, and what and how they learn, in our classrooms and out. That's our focus in Chapter 4. Our initial mirror is fear. Underlying this chapter is our assumption that in our learning and our search for ourselves, as teacher, writer, or student, we're often paralyzed by fear: the fear of being discovered for the frauds we "know" we are, the fear of failure, or of success, and the fear of being known or of not being known. In this chapter we want to create a space that will help people move past their fears and find their authentic selves.

In Chapter 4, expecting that our classrooms reveal our core values and process, we begin there and ask: What is it we're doing in our classrooms, and why? To explore that question, we take you to visit several classrooms, each a different nightmare, and ask you to pause to look at the dispositions[7] of those classrooms and to reflect on your experiences there. Which do you fear most?

What are the dispositions we want present in our own classrooms, and how can we help establish and sustain them? As an entry point, we also include several stories describing classroom practices that, if they do not eliminate, at least have reduced the paralyzing fear that teachers and students can feel.

Since we think you'll benefit from visiting several classrooms and institutions, in this Chapter, rather than creating a single narrative, we focus on several individual stories.

To reflect on our teaching, we also need to reflect on our students: who are they are authentically? We ask this question, because we know that what and how a student learns are inextricably intertwined with who she is. As Parker Palmer puts it, "... there is a deep yearning among students and teachers today—a yearning for embodied meaning—that will be fulfilled only as education embraces the fact that what is inward and invisible is at least as important as what is outward and empirical."*[8] Yet in the current educational environment, we wonder if students (and teachers) are encouraged to bring what they know and what they care about to their work. That leads us to ask what it would mean for a student (or teacher) to be who they are in this environment? What would our teaching look like if we were to meet all the individual needs of our students?

This section also includes the voices of several students, writing about themselves and about their learning. What they write reveals personal dimensions that their teachers and fellow students may not know, several of which are startling. What would a classroom more open to those dimensions look like?

We want our students to learn discerning judgment, yet the judgmental atmosphere that can penetrate our classrooms may mean that students will be overly cautious in exercising their judgment and learning from their mistakes. Because we think it central to both learning and teaching, we return to the theme of teaching non-judgmentally and offer several strategies for doing that.

Chapter 5 invites us to reflect on teaching as a vocation: what it means to be a professional, and what it might mean to have a vocation as a teacher. As with students, our operating assumption is that in the various fora in which a teacher teaches, her teaching is inextricably intertwined with who she is. To help you begin your exploration, we include a professor's story illustrating how challenging it can be to assert and sustain an identity and a voice in a (professional) world that seems consistently threatened by identi-

---

    * Compare Mary Rose O'Reilley:
       Most work of consciousness happens in an underground storehouse
       that mind can only fertilize like a good gardener.
Mary Rose O'Reilley, *The Peaceable Classroom* (Portsmouth, NH: Boynton/ Cook, 1993), 38.

PREFACE xxi

ties that differ from a perceived norm. At the center of the chapter is an essay we have written on vocation. We draw on several sources and offer four exercises for exploring your vocation: writing your obituary or eulogy, finding a governing metaphor, composing a job description, and visiting with your future self. We examine the relationship between vocation and spirituality and include an extended meditation on how we can nurture our vocation, drawing on "processes we can trust," both external and internal. To illustrate those processes, we feature several stories. Finally, we look at two particular elements of a teacher's vocation, writing and classroom teaching, and also offer our perspective on nurturing vocation in our students.

As we began with *Saying Hello*, we end in Chapter 6 with *Saying Goodbye*. We think saying goodbye is an important dimension of our work as teachers. As with hellos, a teacher says many goodbyes, and they rarely are easy. In this chapter you'll find several meditations on saying goodbye.

With these goodbyes, we intend to signal both a form of closure to the retreat inside the book and to invite a form of re-entry into the world.

In an Appendix to the book we include a collection of selected *Resources for Reflecting*. We hope that along with the book, you'll find those resources helpful to you in reflecting on your life as a teacher or in facilitating reflection workshops you might decide to offer your colleagues. We wish you hours of abundant reflection and would be delighted to learn of your experiences using the book or resources and delighted to learn of others you've found helpful.

J.K.P. and M.W.

Notes

1. Parker J. Palmer, Foreword to *Radical Presence: Teaching as Contemplative Practice*, by Mary Rose O'Reilley (Portsmouth, NH: Boynton/Cook, 1998), ix.

2. The Retreat was held at the *Sleeping Lady Resort* in Leavenworth, Washington, accessed January 24, 2011, http://www.sleepinglady.com, and was sponsored by the Institute for Law Teaching and Learning, housed at Gonzaga Law School in Spokane, Washington, accessed January 24, 2011, http://www.law.gonzaga.edu/Centers-Programs/inst_law_teaching-learning.asp.

3. We describe this event more fully in Chapter 2.

4. This Retreat was held in the Canadian Rockies at the Banff Centre in Banff, Alberta, and was organized by Tim Pychyl of the Institute for the Advancement of Teaching in Higher Education, with generous financial support from the publishing company, McGraw-Hill Ryerson.

5. Jennifer Louden, *The Woman's Retreat Book* (San Francisco: Harper, 2004), 28.

6. Mary Rose O'Reilley, *The Peaceable Classroom* (Portsmouth, NH: Boynton/Cook, 1993), xvii.

7. We borrow the term from Stephen Brookfield and Stephen Preskill's discussion in "The Dispositions of Democratic Discussion." *Discussion as a Way of Teaching* (San Francisco: Jossey-Bass, 1999), 8–18.

8. Parker J. Palmer, Foreword to *Radical Presence: Teaching as Contemplative Practice*, by Mary Rose O'Reilley (Portsmouth, NH: Boynton/Cook, 1998), x.

Gratitudes

In our long journey to this book, we've been blessed with many encouraging and supportive people. First, without Gerry Hess, we never would have begun writing. As head of the Institute for Law School Teaching, Gerry conceived the idea for the first Reflecting on Our Teaching retreat, invited Mark to facilitate it, and encouraged Jean to attend. He conceived the second, this time with both Mark and Jean facilitating. And having helped organize and having participated in both, he suggested we write this book. Not only that, during the past 11 years, he's been consistently helpful, reading drafts, offering suggestions, regularly reflecting with us about our teaching, and fortunately, even connecting us with Carolina Academic Press.

With generous financial assistance from McGraw-Hill Ryerson Canada, Tim Pychyl was instrumental in conceiving and organizing our third retreat and has been an enthusiastic supporter throughout. Along with Tim, other colleagues and friends have read and commented wisely on ideas from or drafts of some or all chapters. For that we're grateful to Madelon Baranoski, Kim Brooks, Sue Bryant, Alice Dueker, Liz Karns, Christopher Knapper, Linda Ross Meyer, Susan Olding, and Robert Post.

We've been helped enormously by the hard work and suggestions of several research assistants: Norma Barrett, at Queen's, and Michael L. Brown, Deanna Barkett, David Bartels, Will Bowen, Emma Grunberg, Kathy Hunt, Kabrina Kau, Martha Lovejoy, Aaron Scherzer, Tim Vander Kamp, Will Collins, Scarlet Kim, Rupali Sharma, and Antonio Sanchez at Yale. Camilla Tubbs, Ryan Harrington, and Fred Shapiro at the Lillian Goldman Law Library at Yale provided extraordinary research support.

xxiv GRATITUDES

For their generous financial and logistical support, and research assistance, we're grateful to Yale Law School and Queen's University Law School.

We're grateful to Stephen L. Carter for permission to include a passage from his novel, *The Emperor of Ocean Park*, and to the President and Fellows of Harvard College for permission to include a chapter from Patricia Williams's *The Alchemy of Race and Rights: Diary of a Law Professor*.

Thanks also to Steve Ellmann and the participants in Clinical Theory Workshop for inviting us to present "Experiments in Listening," and for their helpful comments following the presentation, as well as the Law Faculties at Roger Williams University College of Law and CUNY Law School, who gave very helpful feedback when Jean presented ideas from Chapter 3.

We want to acknowledge the work of three people whose secretarial work and was invaluable, and who performed it with patience and grace: Deborah Tropiano at Yale, and Sharron Sluiter and Natalie Moniz-Henne at Queen's.

Finally, we want to acknowledge two groups: the thoughtful teachers who attended our retreats and our incomparable students, who've inspired us and from whom we've learned much of what's in this book. Particular thanks go to those colleagues and students whose work appears in this book: Katie Pratt, Sophie Sparrow, Tom Haffie, Lisa Fong, Tanya Munro, and Stephanie Mah.

Mark also would like to specially acknowledge three people: Don Finkel, without whose years of friendship, curiosity, conversation, insight, and approach to teaching and to life, he would not have been able to grow as a teacher and a person; his wife Susan Olding, for her gifts of love, constant support, encouragement, and patience, and for her model of what means to be a writer and a parent; and finally, to Jean, for a wonderful 11 years of listening, talking, commiserating, laughing …

Jean is grateful to her partners in reflection: Jim, Liz, and Chris Peters, her daily interlocutors; and her other regular interlocutors: Mark, Sue Bryant, Muneer Ahmad, Jeff Selbin, Laurel Fletcher, Mike Wishnie, Alice Dueker and Ann Shalleck.

A Teacher's Reflection Book

Chapter 1

How Does a Teacher Say Hello?

Breakfast was over, and the sunlight streamed through the picture windows framing the view of the Canadian Rockies. As the teachers entered the high vaulted room, they encountered a table strewn with ribbons, yarns, and string of all lengths, widths, and colors, and a card with the following instruction: *Cut a length of ribbon/yarn/twine of your choice and bring it to your seat.* They chatted, looked at the huge binders they had been given at registration. Two minutes after the appointed starting time, they were welcomed by the retreat-sponsoring agency and Mark. "To get us going, take three minutes," he said, "and jot down whatever you would like to say about what you're looking forward to during this retreat and what you're fearful of."

If you like, do the same right now. What are you looking forward to as you begin this book, and what are you concerned about?

Jean then asked the group to take their ribbon and tie a knot in it for the each of the main issues they hoped to address at the retreat. Next she asked them to attach the knotted ribbon to their name tag.

Perhaps you'd like in some way to mark beginning this book, either as Jean suggested above, or with an object or an activity of your own. If so, this might be a good time to do so.

Mark then suggested to the group that as a way of entering the retreat and getting their thinking and writing muscles warmed up, they turn to the quotes that appear below and work with them for several minutes. We invite you to do the same. Please read these five quotes; take your time as you do.

4   1 · HOW DOES A TEACHER SAY HELLO?

White Space[1]

It requires a long time to take in a few words.

On either side of the word we need a patch of white, of silence, like the white space that defines a Chinese painting, or the rests in music that permit the notes to be heard. By and large, our students are relentlessly over stimulated. They sing the body electric: plugged in, tuned out, motorized. And we are over stimulated, too. Many of us hate silence, especially in the classroom. It is the teacher's ultimate nightmare: what if I can't fill fifty minutes? And yet, if students spend twenty minutes in silence looking at ten lines of Homer, it can be time well spent.

I heard a student talking the other day about the difference between two sociology professors. "I love Professor Jones. He lectures from the moment he enters the room, without ever looking at his notes. You really get your money's worth in there. I don't know about Professor Smith. Sometimes you ask him a question and he looks out the window for a while before he answers."

The Teacher Within[2]

When we listen primarily to what we ought to be doing with our lives, we may find ourselves hounded by external expectations that can distort our identity and integrity ... In contrast ... Frederick Buechner offers a more generous and humane image of vocation as "the place where your deep gladness and the world's deep hunger meet."

In a culture that sometimes equates work with suffering, it is revolutionary to suggest that that the best inward sign of vocation is deep gladness—revolutionary but true. If a work is mine to do, it will make me glad over the long haul, despite the difficult days ... If a work does not gladden me in these ways, I need to consider laying it down.

1 · HOW DOES A TEACHER SAY HELLO? 5

An Experiment in Friendship[3]

Attention: deep listening. People are dying in spirit for lack of it. In academic culture most listening is critical listening. We tend to pay attention only long enough to develop a counterargument; we critique the student's or the colleague's ideas; we mentally grade and pigeonhole each other. In society at large, people often listen with an agenda, to sell or petition or seduce. Seldom is there a deep, openhearted, unjudging reception of the other. And so we all talk louder and more stridently and with a terrible desperation. By contrast, if someone truly listens to me, my spirit begins to expand.

The Cloister and the Heart[4]

Human beings, no matter what their background, need to feel that they are safe to open themselves to transformation. They need to feel a connection between a given subject matter and who they are in order for knowledge to take root. That security and connectedness are seldom present in a classroom that recognizes the students' cognitive capacities alone. People often assume that attention to the emotional lives of students, to their spiritual yearnings and their imaginative energies, will somehow inhibit the intellect's free play, drown it in a wash of sentiment, or deflect it into realms of fantasy and escape, that the critical and analytical faculties will be muffled, reined in, or blunted as a result. I believe the reverse is true.

The Danger of Softness[5]

Teachers do teach what they are as much as what they know.

As you read, did one particular quote catch your attention? Choose one and reread it carefully. Take out your journal or a pad, open a document, or use the endpapers of this book. Write for five minutes, responding to the quote. Whatever comes to mind. Just keep your pen moving—don't worry about polish or spelling; just try to get your thoughts down.

After five minutes, check in with yourself. Do you want to write more? By all means, continue until you feel the need to stop.

Next consider this question: Why did you pick up this book? What do you hope to gain by joining us in these reflections? Continue writing, first for five minutes, and then for as long as seems right. If you run out of time, but want to continue, identify a time when you can pick up where you left off, and note it in your calendar.

You'll notice that throughout the book, we'll often invite you to write. We do that so often, because we understand writing to be an important form of thinking; to write concretizes your thinking, makes it more present to you, and often, helps sustain your engagement. However, we understand that you may not have hours at your disposal. But even when we've had only five minutes, we've found that with pen in hand, we often discover more than we would without one, and generate more material for reflection than we otherwise would.

Of course, our welcome to you isn't the only kind you or your students might receive. Imagine yourself seated in *this* room:

> Harry [Potter] had been quite right to think [Professor Minerva McGonagall] wasn't a teacher to cross. Strict and clever, she gave them a talking-to the moment they sat down in her first class.
>
> "Transfiguration is some of the most complex and dangerous magic you will learn at Hogwarts," she said. "Anyone messing around in my class will leave and not come back. You have been warned."
>
> Then she changed her desk into a pig and back again. They were all very impressed and couldn't wait to get started, but soon realized they weren't going to be changing the furniture into animals for a long time. After taking a lot of complicated notes, they were each given a match and started trying to turn it into a needle. By the end of the lesson, only Hermione Granger had made any difference to her match;

1 · HOW DOES A TEACHER SAY HELLO?

Professor McGonagall showed the class how it had gone all silver and pointy and gave Hermione a rare smile.

—J.K. Rowling, *Harry Potter and the Philosopher's Stone*[6]

How would you feel walking out of that room? Intrigued? Intimidated? Anxious to return? Wishing Minerva McGonagall would turn *herself* into a more docile creature?

How do *our* students feel as they leave our introductory classes? Do we know? Would it be useful to find out?

How do *we* feel when we leave?

That first hello isn't the only one we say. As teachers we say many, and they aren't always easy. When we meet each student for the first time—in class, in group settings, or sometimes individually—our hello is an opportunity. Whether momentous, memorable, or mundane, this hello sends many formative messages to a student: messages about the subject matter, the learning process, the dispositions of that classroom, the teacher's regard for the student, the teacher's identity and values.

Throughout a course, we also say micro-hellos—setting the stage at each encounter with signals of welcome or impatience, engagement, or apathy. Some of these tiny hellos precede the first class— perhaps an opening email, a posted announcement, a posted syllabus. Our power in the teacher-student relationship infuses even these micro-signals with meaning, and it can color how a student learns. If the "hello" itself models and embodies that teacher's fundamental values, she already has begun to perform her message and helped set the tone and the parameters for the semester to come.

We say these hellos whether we plan them or not. Even those who doubt the significance of welcome and introduction must acknowledge that "simply getting down to business" itself sends a message: we have work to do; let's get on with it; catch on as quickly as you can.

Professor McGonagall's terse, intensely focused introductory class communicated a world of values to her young first year students: I will tolerate no nonsense; I have mastery in my field; my field is exciting, important, and fascinating; I will excite you with what's possible. You are headed towards a world of new learning

8   1 · HOW DOES A TEACHER SAY HELLO?

and abilities. You will be offered theory and practice. You are just
at the beginning. Success and hard work will be rewarded. Your
progress will delight me.

Since we say these hellos regularly, and since they offer so much
opportunity for holistic communication about the learning to come,
we ought to be aware of the dynamics and components of hello and
be intentional about each encounter. As teachers, we want to make
our first encounters meaningful, to be both inviting and challenging, engaging, possibly even provocative. Through exercises, readings, and questions, the sections below invite you first, to reflect on
how you structure your beginnings. They then explore the functions
of a teacher's hello, and next, its components. The chapter also offers examples of hello and invites you to reflect on the messages you
send, intentionally and inadvertently, in *your* hellos.

I. A Look at Several First Classes

Consider your most recent first class or first teaching encounter
with a group of students. Take a moment to recall how you structured that encounter. What was your to-do list? Perhaps you had
a lesson plan. Here's the one Jean and Mark prepared for the opening session of their first retreat.*

Banff First Plenary

<u>Instruction as walk in</u>: cut a length of ribbon/yarn/twine
of your choice and bring it to your seat

I. MW—*32 minutes*

start within *2 minutes*

Tim—brief welcome—*2 mins*

Mark—warmup—*3 mins*—loud: jot down: what you're
looking forward to, what you're fearful of—jkp: rib-
bon/tie the knot and tie the ribbon

---

*   The parenthetical passages weren't in the original; we've included them
to clarify several of our shorthand expressions.

Mark—(Retreat materials) tab 7: quotes (five quotations, reproduced above)—*25 mins*

10 mins for reading and writing: *5 mins* to read them/pick one that resonates strongly

spend time writing about it—*7 mins*

6 mins: turn to neighbor and talk about what you've written

have space for debriefing—*6 mins*

consider whether groups of two with one three (Jean as part of the three)

4 mins: take a few comments about what came up

II. JKP—introductions—*40 mins*

(each person interview and introduces another)
Something new and good in your life right now

10 mins: 5 mins each way (for interviewing)—Jean timer

15 mins: 25 × 30 seconds; have Katie or Lily start—ring chime at 30 seconds (Tim? or Lily?)(time with palm)

(Discussion)
what did we just do?

interviewed

were interviewed

describing someone

hearing self described

hearing others described

jean should watch her humor issues

hook—were you uncomfortable sharing much? teaching who you are is critical theme of the retreat.

how do we get to the place where we truly know who our students are and who we are—and do we want to go there?

III. MW *18 mins*—Retreat Introduction

overview of retreat (mw): focus on reflection; try to create spaces; variety of strategies; time to pursue what interests you; we're flexible, available, and will check in; it's *your* retreat; announcements (jkp)/keeping to time (to allow day-

10   1 · HOW DOES A TEACHER SAY HELLO?

light time)/ start on time—**PowerPoint**—schedule (mw—
jkp writes) (rhythm of plenaries and small groups)/an-
nouncements (laptop)—jkp announce that ground rules
get posted in this room **Before lunch**; homework—first
night—IRE; second night—Williams, Materials, Tab 31
and intro to small groups/individual reflection event (explained in Chapter 2)
Round? Roll it Over—be flexible

What do *your* lesson plans look like? More structured? Less?
Take a moment to recall a lesson plan and the class itself. Did
it go as you planned? Did some events take longer? Did others get
cut? Take a moment to jot down memories from the actual class.

For another example, here are Jean's notes preparing her first
class in a seminar.

Advocacy for Children and Youth:
Fall 2008
Class One—Planning
Thursday, September 4, 12:10–2, Room 111

Time	What?	Computer needs	What to Bring?	Who?
12:10	*Professional Responsibility Riot Act—how clinic and representing clients is a paradigm shift from studies*		notes	JKP
12:20	*Thing of Beauty*	Projector—in powerpoint —Van Gogh		JKP
12:25	*LSO Announcements*			KJ
12:30	*Introductions Exercise with debriefing*—4 law students, JKP, Deb—each student interviews a stranger (10 mins); each person introduces someone to the class (45 secs each)		Chime; timer; notepad; checklist	All, led by JKP

1:10	*Announcements* • *Thing of Beauty Signup (everyone needs to sign up 2 or 3 times)* • *ACY Blackboard page (all have access?)* • *ACY research site* • *CCPA forms* • *Going through the Syllabus—odd dates* • *Explaining the timing of the two cases*		TOB signup sheet (extra copy of syllabus)	JKP
1:25	*Choosing partners/BREAK*			Students —all else step out
1:35	*Introduction to Neglect Proceedings and our Role*	PowerPoint chart		JKP
1:50	*Case Assignments/ First meetings scheduling*	Team I: petition/list/ goals memo Team II Goals memos (4)		JKP and all Super- vising students

Here are Jean's reflections on this class, after she taught it.

Went very much according to plan. The second to last item, Introduction to Neglect Proceedings, was truncated, as it almost always is.

I remember during the announcements going through the complicated question of scheduling and assigning their first cases. This seemed to go particularly well, in that the students seemed to fully understand the process—I felt that not only was I being transparent about how they would get their cases and when they would be busy, but also that they were truly engaged in taking it in. (This has varied **widely** in the past; I think this year, looking at the calendar created on the Inside Page (Online Blackboard Site) together may have made the difference.)

Students were quite quiet. One student was quite active, and made reference to class readings which had not yet been assigned (had read ahead in the book). This seemed to silence the other three students even more. Students generally deferred to my plan for the class and were quite compliant. Students were somewhat hard to read. I already knew one of the four students, but didn't know the others at all; the one I knew was also very quiet. I felt very aware that she had already taken a different clinic class with me in which the first class had been similarly structured; in fact, I had talked to her about the fact that, in setting up this class schedule, I had deliberately left in some repetitive materials because I thought that repeating them in the new setting could be enlightening to her. Still, I felt somewhat self-conscious that one person was repeating things (like the introductions exercise) while others were thrown in for the first time.

What are your reflections on a recent first class? Take some time to gather your thoughts and write them down.

Consider how satisfied you were with that first encounter? Are you planning to structure things similarly the next time around? Jot down some recollections and thoughts for your next first class.

Here's Jean again.

As often happens, the students left looking, to me, both excited and scared. That made sense to me, because I knew that they had understood the amount of work that was coming at them. They also looked motivated to put in the time and effort that would be required to do the work well. I felt helpless to prevent the nearly certain experience of feeling lost and overwhelmed that the early weeks would evoke; I warned them about it, but wasn't sure that would help them when they actually hit the wall.

I also found myself terribly put off by the laptops in the class. Amid their quietness, the students were very engaged in their computers, but less in conversation. Plan to consider strongly discouraging students from using laptops next semester.*

Finally, think about what you're trying to communicate, to embody, in your hellos. For you, what makes a successful beginning? If you feel clear about the answers to these questions, and comfortable with how your hellos are proceeding in practice, you may not want to spend much more time in this chapter. We've designed it as an invitation to consider the role of hello in the integral structure of your teaching. If you have a clear sense of this, and are satisfied with how these hellos work, you probably have a good answer to the question: "As a teacher, how do I say Hello?"

The remainder of this chapter offers reflections about beginnings. We invite you to read on, hoping you will find that our thoughts help you to consolidate and refine your own deeply felt intuitions and experiences.

II. Exercises to Focus on Hello

To help you continue your reflections on your hellos, consider the following exercises. Again, go with whatever ideas spark your thinking.

---

* After this concern about laptops kept appearing in Jean's written reflections and discussions with colleagues and experienced students, she decided to add a piece to the opening class, stating her expectation that laptops will only be used in class to aid the students' understanding of the seminar or progress on behalf of her client case work. Jean has found that this has largely resolved her concerns about laptops taking away from the quality of conversation or community building in the class.

Mark has found that negotiating a class laptop protocol has worked well to encourage students to remain committed to it.

14   1 · HOW DOES A TEACHER SAY HELLO?

A. What Is the First Experience Students Have in Your Course? What Is Their First Experience in Class?

Here's an example from one of Mark's courses. It's called Images of Doctors and Lawyers in Literature and includes students from both law and medical schools. Mark begins first, by postponing introductions and then inviting the class to read aloud a story. Mark and his medical school co-teachers chose a play written early in the 20th Century: *A Jury of Her Peers*.[7] They had annotated the play, indicating five speaking parts and a "narrator." Students volunteer for the five main parts, and everyone else reads as the narrator, with each person reading one paragraph. In this way, everyone's voice is present in the room. And since those voices do not represent any student's authentic voice or thinking, no one is singled out or on the spot.

Of course, to be asked to read aloud on the first day of an upper year graduate course can be disorienting, but students usually embrace their roles vigorously.

The story concerns an investigation of the death of a man living with his wife in an isolated area outside a small town. His wife was with him when he died, and the town prosecutor, sheriff, and another man come to investigate. Two of the men have brought their wives. While the men search the house for clues, the women remain in the kitchen, and as they look around, they discover a clue that would implicate the wife. At the end of the story, rather than reveal this crucial evidence, they hide it. Hence the title.

Following the reading, the students break into mixed groups of four or five, discuss the story, and then return for a plenary discussion. Using the small groups provides another low risk environment, encouraging everyone to participate, so that when the class begins its plenary discussion, people typically are engaged and energized, and they participate vigorously. That sets the scene and the rhythm for the following classes.

While this class is seminar size, Mark uses a similar strategy in a much larger course. Reading proceeds around the room, each person reading a paragraph. Not everyone will read, but the subsequent group and plenary discussions are similarly vigorous.

When Jean works with classes of 100 or more, she limits each reader to one sentence, and when the reading is finished, notes that all voices now have entered the room.

If you prefer to begin your course with introductions, consider asking your students to introduce themselves, including in those introductions "something new and good in their lives right now." Their contributions often are amusing and can help relax what often are tense opening moments. Mark remembers one male student offering: "Last Christmas I went to my boyfriend's house for dinner, and for the first time in six years his mother didn't have a migraine."

B.   What Are the Dispositions of Your Classroom?

Whether consciously, inadvertently, or by some mixture of the two, teachers initially structure a space for learning. Over the span of any learning experience, this space evolves dynamically, sometimes predictably, but equally often taking forms we neither could anticipate nor control. Can you remember a learning environment that miraculously flourished and bore fruit, almost magically? Can you remember another that despite thoughtful planning, spiraled downward, seemingly without any hope of redemption? Looking back, can you identify any of the factors that might have led to these experiences?

How would you describe the learning space you want to create in your classroom, both physical and psychic? For example, where it's possible, Mark often reconfigures a classroom space to have groups of students sitting around tables, facing each other. Alternatively, as he's described above, he'll ask students to form small discussion groups, sometimes at their fixed seats, sometimes by moving to differing spaces in the room.

What is your image of the community you hope will emerge during the course, and how might you foster it? Stephen Brookfield describes how in his courses, he begins almost immediately working on building a community, asking his students to reflect on the best and worst conversations they've encountered, note

16   1 · HOW DOES A TEACHER SAY HELLO?

what contributed to each, and then suggest, first individually, and then in the group, the elements that would contribute to constructing what he calls a "democratic classroom." This "ground rules" exercise takes time, but can help foster a cooperative environment for all the discussions to come.[8]

Brookfield and his colleague Stephen Preskill have suggested that such a community should embrace and exemplify the following values.[9]

THE DISPOSITIONS OF A DEMOCRATIC CLASSROOM

Hospitality
Participation
Mindfulness
Humility
Mutuality
Deliberation
Appreciation
Hope
Autonomy

Would these dispositions work for you? Would you adopt any as your own? If so, how would you plan to implement/embody them? If not, what would you substitute?

C. Fast Forward Through the Semester You're about to Start

It is the last class; it has been a great semester. What is the feeling in the room? What were the interactions like? What is being discussed? What does a great ending tell you about its beginning? (By the way—do you have an idea for how to run that ending class, or an explicit way to link that class to this first one, creating bookends for the course?)

D. Consider "Entrainment" and the Rhythms of Your Semester

Dr. Stephan Rechtschaffen, one of the founders of the Omega Institute for Holistic Studies, notes that all creatures *entrain* with the rhythms in their environment: heartbeats align, menstrual cycles coincide, feet tap to music. "We are creatures of habit who have become habituated to society's pulse."[10] Rechtschaffen urges us to remember that "life itself—time itself—is the unfolding of ... myriad ... rhythms." Since much entrainment is reactive, timeshifting requires us to become conscious and responsible, proactive about the rhythms with which we entrain.

As you and your students come together from disparate contexts and preoccupations, to spend a semester or a year in collaboration, what rhythms will you be inviting them, and modeling for them, to adopt? Even when we don't feel quite ready for the hubbub of a semester, its beginning places special burdens on us to lead the way, setting the new rhythm for starting work.

E. Think about Hellos in Popular Culture

Can you remember a great beginning of a movie, a play, a song, a novel, which swept you up into its experience? Consider, for instance, the majestic start to the *Lion King* movie and play, in which all the animals of the kingdom slowly gather and cross the plain to witness the blessing of Simba, the newborn heir? Or "the best of times, the worst of times" from Dickens's, *A Tale of Two Cities*? If you find a hello that made a strong impression on you, try breaking it down. What specifically made the impact— the words? the setting? What created the space that you wanted to enter?

F. How Will You Deal with Fluctuating Student Attendance During "Shopping Periods"?

If, like us, you struggle with "shopping periods," during which students try out the course and the roster fluctuates, consider the strategy adopted by Bill Watterson. For years Watterson wrote a Sunday version of *Calvin and Hobbes* that he sent to two different kinds of newspapers—those that published the cartoon in three rows of panes, with the title pane and one or two others on the top row, and those who could publish only two rows, with the title running along the side. Every week, Watterson had to envision a beginning to the cartoon, which enhanced its meaning, but could also be lopped off without disrupting the cartoon.[11] How could you preview the essential elements of your course authentically, but also in a way that would enable a latecomer to benefit fully without those opening beats?

G. What Will Be the Role of Technology in Your Classroom, and Will You Make Space to Express That in Your Hello?

Will you be dimming the lights, showing PowerPoints, splicing in video clips, even music? Will you want your students on laptops during class? What do you envision as the role of technology in your teaching space, and how will you introduce it?

H. Will You Know Your Students' Names?

From research we've learned that knowing your students' names has a disproportionately positive influence on relationships in the classroom. Do you usually know your students' names? How quickly? How do you learn them?

Consider one unorthodox idea. Our friend, Gerry Hess, regularly teaches first year procedure classes of seventy or more, often two sections at a time. One first day assignment to students sends them to a room in which a video camera is set up and on pause: they are asked to turn on the camera, stand before it, say their name, and

1 · HOW DOES A TEACHER SAY HELLO?   19

say one additional thing about themselves: "I am Jean Koh Peters and I love to quilt." Gerry watches the composite tape over lunch for the first week or so, until the names start naturally coming to him in class—"Aren't you Ms. Clark, who just got certified in Scuba?"

I.   How Will You Handle Your Announcements?

First day announcements can number in the dozens, but they can bore students, who then forget them. How can you help the students remember what is important for early days in the course? Consider projecting or circulating a semester calendar for time oriented information; the role of humor; a handout or email summarizing the info. What are other ideas for making announcements work?

As you do this, consider what you are assuming your students already know—about the material, about you, about the school's academic culture? Are some students better situated to know these things than others? Could students from diverse backgrounds be hamstrung if certain core ideas, values, or histories are not made explicit? Be careful when you assume "everyone knows" particular background information, and consider those who might not.

J.   As You Begin, How Do You Want the Central Ideas of the Course to Emerge?

As we began this book, Mark and I detected a consistent difference of style between us. At any moment, Jean was much more likely to want her messages to be transparent and explanatory, while Mark preferred to let the messages emerge over time, implicitly. For all the teaching decisions this book will prompt you to reflect upon, this dimension will remain an additional decision point. Will you be overt about your hello, or let it happen without comment? Remember, the most carefully planned hello may never refer to that concept; the most explicit hello may not be the most thoughtful. Do you naturally gravitate to one approach or find yourself on some other point on the spectrum between them? When should you disrupt that natural tendency?

20   1 · HOW DOES A TEACHER SAY HELLO?

K. Consider Generating Ideas by Using Beginning Rituals in Other Settings

How does your yoga class start? Your church service? Your favorite sports commentary show? Would your teaching setting benefit from a ritual opening?

Jean traditionally begins her classes with a "thing of beauty," brought by someone in the class, including a faculty member. The guidelines for the thing of beauty: the presentation must take five minutes or less and consist of something which the presenter considers beautiful. Over the years, Jean, her colleagues, and her students have brought: music (some performed live), videos, PowerPoint shows of photos and art, their own creations (crocheted blankets, etchings, quilts), cherished gifts, blogposts, comic books, baked or cooked goods, poetry, and many other varied items.

Would the space created in your class by a ritual beginning in your class help promote the values you are seeking?

III. Final Thoughts about Hello

Saying Hello serves some critical framing functions, which may help some teachers think through their approach to beginnings. Here are a few thoughts. Of course, there are no right or wrong approaches, only choices you must make about the messages you wish to send as you begin.

The hello has the primacy effect. First impressions carry a lot of weight in teaching. Your choices in how you first encounter the class may implicitly send multiple messages about your values, the classroom atmosphere and learning environment, and your teaching goals.

The hello can offer an overview of the learning experience. Students naturally seek to grasp what the course will cover and exclude, and what they might expect to learn during the semester or year. They also want to know their workload, how they will be asked to participate, and what a successful student needs to do.

1 · HOW DOES A TEACHER SAY HELLO? 21

The hello can demonstrate the methods of the course. The form of opening classes may make an implicit promise about future sessions. For instance, an initial lecture suggests more of the same for later classes, and an expected role of listening and absorption by the students throughout the course.*

The hello can frame the teacher-student relationship. A teacher's hello can set roles for teacher and student. It can encourage or discourage out of class contact; it can set an expectation for teacher feedback on student work. It can begin a dialogue with the class about its format and procedures.

The hello's multiple messages can align or contradict each other. A hello whose messages align seems to have the greatest impact in the shortest time.

The best hellos can prefigure the best goodbyes.

———————

Consider this one last Hello— *"It's all About Me"*

When the whole class was seated, Lockhart cleared his throat loudly and silence fell. He reached forward, picked up Neville Longbottom's copy of **Travels with Trolls***, and held it up to show his own, winking portrait on the front.*

"Me," he said, pointing at it and winking as well. "Gilderoy Lockhart, Order of Merlin, Third Class, Honorary Member of the Dark Force Defense League, and five-time winner of Witch 'Weekly's Most-Charming-Smile Award—but I don't talk about that. I didn't get rid of the Bandon Banshee by smiling at her!" "I see you've all bought a complete set of my books—well done. I thought we'd start today with a little quiz. Nothing to worry about—just to check how well you've read them, how much you've taken in—."

———————

* Borrowing a phrase from Stephen Brookfield, at the end of the first class in one course that he expects students will find unorthodox, Mark distributes a series of "Product Warnings," intended to inform students how the classes will be conducted and what he expects from his students.

Stephen Brookfield and Stephen Preskill, *Discussion as a Way of Teaching: Tools and Techniques for Democratic Classrooms.* (San Francisco: Jossey-Bass, 1999), 61.

22   1 · HOW DOES A TEACHER SAY HELLO?

When he had handed out the test papers he returned to the front of the class and said, "You have thirty minutes ... start —now!"

Harry looked down at his paper and read:

1. *What is Gilderoy Lockhart's favorite color?*
2. *What is Gilderoy Lockhart's secret ambition?*
3. *What, in your opinion, is Gilderoy Lockhart's greatest achievement to date?*

On and on it went, over three sides of paper, right down to:

54. *When is Gilderoy Lockhart's birthday, and what would his ideal gift be?*

Half an hour later, Lockhart collected the papers and rifled through them in front of the class.

"Tut, tut—hardly any of you remembered that my favorite color is lilac. I say so in **Year with the Yeti***. And a few of you need to read* **Wanderings with Werewolves** *more carefully—I clearly state in chapter twelve that my ideal birthday gift would be harmony between all magic and nonmagic peoples—though I wouldn't say no to a large bottle of Ogden's Old Firewhiskey!"*[12]

Parker Palmer has reminded us, again and again, that as teachers, we teach who we are, even when we're trying not to. We bring our values, our commitments, our chosen learning, ourselves, to the classroom. It is therefore understandable, and possibly worrying, that this truth can easily slide into a strong inadvertent message sent in the classroom: that the class is all about the teacher.

Gilderoy Lockhart's comical self-absorption offers a cautionary tale.* Compare Minerva McGonagall's brief display of mastery in her field (turning her desk into a pig) to Lockhart's list of awards and achievements. As we begin with new students, do we struggle with the question of how to establish our expertise in the field?

---

* Too little about me also can be problematic. Reading his student evaluations, Mark often finds several comments from students indicating they'd have preferred him to reveal more of his perspectives.

1 · HOW DOES A TEACHER SAY HELLO?   23

Somehow, we teach who we are, but our teaching is not all about us. How do we manage this? We are perpetually tempted to put ourselves in the center of our teaching, because our self is indeed integral to what we teach and how we decide to teach it. If we imagine a spectrum, the left pole being the concept "its all about me" and the right being the concept "my teaching has nothing to do with me," there probably is no place in quality teaching for either pole. We risk Gilderoy Lockhart's self-unawareness on the left side, but the right also has its perils: an arid, also self-unaware focus on subject matter alone, separated from the human engagement of learning.

IV. Conclusion

One morning you wake up and realize that the hello is over. You are smack in the middle of the semester. You are no longer struggling with student's names; the classroom rings with conversation steeped in context and group identity; and collaborations fruitfully begun pile their notes all over your desk and computer desktop. It is both a relief and a loss to leave the hello behind: relief from the unknowing, the diving in, the shifting gears into meeting and greeting mode; loss, as that activation energy fades in the subsequent long days and shorter breaks in the action, and the excitement of the new yields to the daily slog of mid-semester.

Perhaps this also is a good time to reflect. Did my hello lay the groundwork for relationships—with my students, with my colleagues, at home—that reflect the values of the work? As my initial energy ebbs, can I commit to the values, not the fatigue or the overstimulation, framing my actions and articulating my thoughts? Are any of us giving ourselves credit for how the toll that hitting the ground running on Day 1 of every semester feels on Day 30 of the semester?

Thank heavens for "Hello." A time to re-remember why we are doing what we are doing. A touchstone in more ordinary times.

Notes

1. Mary Rose O'Reilley, *The Peaceable Classroom* (Portsmouth, NH: Boynton/Cook, 1993), 105.

2. Parker J. Palmer, *The Courage to Teach: Exploring the Inner Landscape of a Teacher's Life* (San Francisco: Jossey-Bass, 1998), 30.

3. Mary Rose O'Reilley, *Radical Presence: Teaching as a Contemplative Practice* (Portsmouth, NH: Boynton/Cook, 1998), 19.

4. Jane Tompkins, *A Life in School: What the Teacher Learned* (Reading, MA: Addison Wesley, 1996), 213.

5. Peter Elbow, *What is English* (New York: Modern Language Association of America, 1990), 205.

6. J.K. Rowling, *Harry Potter and the Philosopher's Stone* (New York: Scholastic, 1997), 134.

7. Susan Glaspell, "A Jury of Her Peers," in *The Best American Short Stories of the Century*, ed. John Updike (Boston: Houghton Mifflin, 1999).

8. Stephen Brookfield, "Creating Ground Rules for Critical Conversation," in *Becoming a Critically Reflective Teacher* (San Francisco: Jossey-Bass, 1993), 143–45.

9. Excerpted from Brookfield and Preskill, *Discussion as a Way of Teaching*, 8–18.

10. Stephan Rechtschaffen, *Timeshifting: Creating More Time to Enjoy Your Life* (New York: Doubleday, 1996), 30.

11. Bill Watterson, *Calvin and Hobbes: Sunday Pages 1985–1995* (Kansas City: Andrews McNeel, 2001), 13–14.

12. J.K. Rowling, *Harry Potter and The Chamber of Secrets* (Vancouver: Raincoast, 1999), 77–78.

Chapter 2

Reflection: What It Is and How to Practice It

I. Introduction: A Reflection on the Need for Reflection

As we've prepared and facilitated these retreats and begun writing this book, we've heard from many people who long, not only for a chance to reflect on their rich and challenging experiences teaching, but also for the assurance that they will have a chance to reflect regularly. Often this longing echoes other longings: for a chance to slow down, for a regular exercise routine, for time and space to do what seems really important, rather than careening throughout the day from email to meeting to class to crisis. People wonder how they can be assured that they always will be able to reflect on their important work and sense that their lives and work would be better for that assurance.

For many of us, our days are full of what we might call non-mindful overactivity. Life has become too much—even if it is too much of a good thing. Crammed with the important, the urgent, there is no space for reflecting, no pause to breathe, to process. A teacher moves from one event, activity, class, meeting, exam, conference, presentation, speech, to another, with constant input, constant output, and no time to take stock.

Even when the pace finally slows, the habits of non-mindfulness can hold fast. Once given time, a teacher—used to speed, efficiency, multi-tasking—does not necessarily use it for reflection. In fact, many teachers experience the transition out of the semester, to summer, or sabbatical, as profoundly disturbing, jolting, boring, or worse. Activities continue at a saner pace, but the habits of non-mindfulness prevail. The mind is still racing, resisting quiet, seeking fresh overstimulation.

Reflecting can provide an ongoing process in which teachers remain learners, learning from their rich experience with students, with the academy, and with their scholarship. In this cycle of teaching and learning, teachers renew their perspectives, redeem mistakes, and continue to develop and mature, no matter how experienced or expert they may be. Reflecting invites us to approach our subject with a beginner's mind, which often leads us to fresh perspectives and renewed energy. Reflecting often restores a fresh dimension to a life that, without time to ponder and catch up, can become flat, routine, drudgery, even to those who love it most. Indeed, many who have come to reflect with us are troubled that their teaching life, which they have long loved, has lost its excitement. And they have lost their commitment. Within minutes of giving themselves space, time, and permission to reflect, they find themselves re-engaged, full of ideas, and able to begin working on pesky recurring problems.

What does it mean to reflect? For us, reflection is an intentional, non-judgmental review of experience. Following Goldsmith, we understand reflection to be "an ongoing conversation with the self, that moves hand in hand with experience."[1] At its best, reflection becomes purposeful, lifelong learning from experience, through witnessing that experience, examining it, illuminating and exploring it. To reflect requires courage and a willingness to look at one's experience honestly and to be open to the lessons it teaches.

We reflect because life goes by too fast. Something rich happens, but we lose the experience before we can understand its true meaning. The time allotted was insufficient, or something else that we had to do confronted us almost immediately. In a life without reflection, meaning vanishes with the moment. Doing has swallowed learning.

Reflection recovers meaning from moments past, in four ways:

1. *Reflection integrates.* As teachers move almost automatically through dozens of tasks each day, a busy, challenging teaching life can become fragmented. We

need to pull together separate experiences, to note how something that happened in one class is connected to what happened in a meeting three days earlier. Reflection allows us to understand our many professional responsibilities as part of a whole that reflects our deepest and most authentic vocation as teachers, scholars, institutional citizens, and colleagues.

2. *Reflection takes stock.* Reflection creates a moment for seeing where we've been, remembering where we are going, and remembering why we are on the road in the first place. In his book *Sabbath*, Wayne Mueller recalls a South American tribe that would walk for days, and then stop, waiting for their "souls to catch up with them."[2] Reflection offers perspective—in the heat of the moment, an article or essay looks as if it's going nowhere; on reflection, in a quiet moment, the writer sees how far she has come. Reflection allow us to step back from doing and remember the why we're doing it, and then, either recommit to the task or revise or abandon it.

3. *Reflection helps us continue our learning as well as our teaching.* As teachers, we constantly are called on to deliver, to offer, to give. Reflection allows us to receive, to absorb, to take from our experience, and in that way to continue growing. In turn, reflection enriches our giving by filling our well with new resources, new ideas, new energy.

4. *Reflection transcends the constraints of action and peer pressure.* As teachers, much of what we do each week with students, staff, and colleagues is public, and consequently, subject to external constraints and pressures. Reflection offers us an opportunity to review those actions away from those external pressures that may have helped shape them.

Our goal is to help you find a practice of reflecting that works for you, by whatever means. We have two practical suggestions. First, developing a practice of mindful reflection can lead to incorporating its benefits into your daily teaching life. Knowing your daily rhythms of work and finding a way to make reflection an ordinary part of your life can enrich your teaching days and continually replenish the well of insight, inspiration, and hope.

Second, during a reflection drought, either when beginning to develop a practice, or when trying to revive a lapsed one, we recommend designing an individual reflection event. This event, described in detail in this chapter, both addresses a specific reflection need, and permits you to try out different modes of reflecting that you may use in your practice. We will suggest detailed ideas for individual reflection events that follow the structure of a retreat or mini-retreat, but again, we care most that you are able to design a fruitful event for yourself, whatever structure you use.

Having identified the benefits of reflection, we now explore its essential elements. Following that, we describe a single planned act of reflection—the individual reflection event. Next, we consider what a practice of mindful reflection, ongoing acts of reflection undertaken over time, might look like. Finally, we explore ways to develop a practice of mindful reflection, including removing barriers and creating conditions conducive to reflection.

We have met many teachers who strongly wish to reflect but find that often they can't make the time, can't make the space, or don't know what to do once they get there. This book is designed to help you get past these three problems.

II. Essential Elements of Reflection— What Makes Reflection Work for You?

Ultimately, you must determine the elements of reflection you find essential. In this section we focus, first, on ways to identify elements that previously have worked for you, and then suggest three critical elements we have found indispensable to reflection.

2 · REFLECTION

A. Identify Meaningful Elements of Reflection That Uniquely Suit Your Needs

Each of us already has a reflective process. Even if nascent, truncated, or long in hibernation, it is likely that something you previously have experienced about reflection has led you to this book. Your first task, then, is to identify specifically what has worked for you when you've reflected previously, and what, to you, defines fruitful reflection.

In Chapter 5, we focus on internal "processes you can trust" that bear fruit, usually in solitude or with deeply trusted others, in aligning your life with your deepest values. These processes often become deeply idiosyncratic as we tailor them, increasingly, to our own preferences. For instance, a scholar who finds coffee shops a productive place for writing may find herself tweaking the setting over time, identifying a perfect nook, her favorite coffee drink, her needed supplies.

Processes you can trust fertilize rich reflection. Here are several ideas for discovering or creating for your daily life internal processes you can trust. As you search your history for elements of reflection, consider the following topics and questions:

1. *Investigate your daily routines and rituals.* During what parts of the day do you find yourself able to access your most authentic thoughts? What times of the day can you rely on to be centered times of constructive thinking? Do you have your best ideas in the shower, or, possibly, loading the dishwasher? Do you have a daily walk to your favorite cafe? Do you have an afternoon run that always gets you out of bad mood?

2. *Identify processes you already can trust.* Can you identify any processes you can trust that you already know "work" for you: mulling over a problem during a brisk run, walking in nature, calling a trusted friend, journaling, meditating? In particular, think of processes that have long been reliable in helping you identify your authentic concerns and aspirations. (Jean remembers a moment writing this chapter during which,

after a writing drought, she was so excited about some ideas that she pulled off the road and reached for her journal, a daily companion for her. She knew it was a good sign!)

3. *Identify trustworthy interlocutors.* Who brings out the best in you? Who are the people who listen well and with whom you feel safe and secure? People who seem to accompany you easily to important, authentic places? If you have obvious candidates, two options follow. Try to spend more time with this person or these people; if the person does not live locally, be creative, exploring regular phone calls, email, internet chatting. And when that isn't possible, create a time of quiet reflection in which you imagine the questions this person might ask if they were available.

4. *Identify the processes you can't trust.* In times when you have failed to reflect fruitfully, what inhibited your process? Are there times of day when you are likely to be frazzled, edgy, impelled by what others expect of you, rather than by your own intrinsic values? Are there times when you find yourself regularly wondering "why on earth am I doing this?" Are there people who regularly bring out the worst in you and your work?

5. *Remember an inspired moment and work backwards to recreate the processes that led to it.* Can you remember one moment or occasion of reflection that was particularly noteworthy? Examine that in depth. What made it fulfilling? What facilitated or frustrated your process?

6. *Beyond specific incidents, remember periods in your life (jobs, school settings, relationships) in which reflection came easily.* In times when you have found yourself reflecting deeply and fruitfully, what supported that process?

7. *Consider adding to your day processes that complement your current routines.* Looking at the whole of your

daily activities—the balance of work and play, the balance of input (reading, lectures, listening) and output (writing, lecturing, opining)—consider what is missing and how it might be added. For instance, if your examination of your daily routine shows that you spend many sedentary hours with others in dialogue, adding a short quiet solitary walk could enhance your process. If you are constantly lecturing and teaching, and rarely reading, can you make reading a focal point for your reflection? Are there processes you've been meaning to try: walking or tracing a labyrinth, a letter to a friend, a support group, tai chi?

In the end, what do these processes yield? At their best, they can keep our eyes on the prize—orient, or reorient, us to vocation before we head back into the world to try to pursue that vocation. At the least, they can help us regroup our energy, get quiet, hear our own thoughts, even regain our sense of humor.

Take a moment now to jot down, in a journal, on a napkin, in the margin of this book, any ideas this section has sparked about your own process. Ask yourself these specific questions:

1. *What makes reflection fruitful for me? (Remember, you are an audience of one—if it works for you, don't worry if no one else understands why.)*

2. *What processes can I trust? What new processes do I want to try?*

B. Three Recommended Elements of Reflection: Starting Focal Point, Experience, Non-judgment

If your previous experiences with reflection do not provide enough ideas about helpful elements for reflecting, consider these three components that our own reflection and our experience at our retreats have led us to recommend:

1. A Starting Focal Point

Reflection focuses on a clear starting point. This may be an event one wishes to understand more deeply and clearly: an intention, which is a frame for the session of reflection; a prompt, which provides an experience to be debriefed in the same or in another session; a reading, with time to discuss it afterwards; a problem, to be solved; a choice to be made; and the like.

Having a starting focal point distinguishes reflection from related activities like meditation and journaling. In meditation, one specifically tries to clear one's mind of thoughts to process, seeking to settle into an awareness of the present moment without processing experiences and thoughts of the past or future. In many forms of journaling and diary keeping,[3] writers are encouraged to use a style of freewriting that drops thoughts on the page without a set focus or direction, following the mind wherever it may lead. While meditation and freewriting may prove to be useful components of a reflection event, especially in their ability to prepare one for reflection, these centering activities are usually not the stuff of reflection itself.

Neglecting to have a clear starting point, or focus, endangers your carefully cultivated time for reflecting. Remember, something about your routine has made it difficult to reflect naturally, leading you to this book and this examination of your teaching life. Without a focal point, your time away from the heat of work could devolve into a continuation of your work dynamics—anxiety, to do list making, critical self-judgment—from which reflection provides a much needed respite. Think of the starting point as the portal into reflection, the fork in the road away from preoccupation with work rhythms and worries and into a place of perspective and non-judgmental thinking.

2. Experience

Reflection has a retrospective center—it reviews the past for lessons, insights, learning. Digesting the rich experiences of teaching and the teaching life, in a process distinct from the preparation that inspired them or the heat of the moment of their execution,

2 · REFLECTION   33

is central to reflection. Reflection allows us to be respectful witnesses and students of our life experience.

In our teaching lives, we often ignore the good moments: the moments when it all feels right, when it moves smoothly. Even those of us with regular reflective practices often focus those on problem spots, debriefing the difficult or trying to avoid similar problems in the future. In a time-starved teaching life, a class that ran smoothly may appear to need no debriefing; we may be tempted to say, "whew, thank God that went all right," and bound forward into our next task. Reflection views all past experience, whether it feels positive, neutral, or negative, as rich fodder for learning and as a gift to the future, helping us learn from our teaching and use those lessons in service of our future students, and selves. In fact, since we often learn better from encouragement, it makes sense to spend time asking what went right, and why.

3. Non-judgment

If reflection has been troublesome for you, it may be helpful to make a key shift in your reflection to a discipline of non-judgment. Cultivate a spirit of non-judgment towards yourself, with a clear sense that you have nothing to prove.

Non-judgment requires an open spirit of inquiry and factfinding, bracketing our impulses to blame, evaluate, judge. From the outset of examining an experience or an event, the reflector decides to maintain an attitude of non-judgment. All observations will be made in terms of facts and details witnessed, rather than conclusions or critiques formulated.

Jean has written about this kind of inquiry with Susan Bryant, in their "five habits of cross-cultural lawyering."[4] Non-judgment is key to each of the five habits, and can be illustrated by the third habit, parallel universe thinking. In parallel universe thinking, rather than quickly, and possibly prematurely, reaching a settled conclusion, a person brainstorms alternative explanations for a set of circumstances.

Looking clearly and non-judgmentally at our past choices may deepen our reflection. It can help us break patterns of self-con-

34   2 · REFLECTION

demnation and self-criticism that can escalate stress in our daily
lives. As Jon Kabat-Zinn notes:

> [m]indfulness is cultivated by assuming the stance of an
> impartial witness to your own experience. To do this re-
> quires that you become aware of the constant stream of
> judging and reacting to inner and outer experiences that
> we are all normally caught up in, and learn to step back
> from it.[5]

The Sufi mystic poet Rumi[6] offers this image for non-judgment:
"Out beyond ideas of wrongdoing and rightdoing, / there is a field.
I'll meet you there." Non-judgmental reflection takes place in that
field.

For instance, imagine that a teacher decides to focus a session
of reflection on a class session in which he suspects something
went awry:

> *Example: I worked hard to prepare a carefully crafted intro-
> duction to the subject matter, which I knew would be chal-
> lenging to the students and which would be our subject for
> the next two months. To introduce this material, I had the
> idea of creating an engaging first five minutes of class. I had
> prepared a PowerPoint presentation with a chart, an outline,
> and even a slide with some jokes on it, but when I looked up,
> the students were all looking at their laptops. When I asked
> for questions, they stared at me with faces I couldn't read, or
> just continued looking at their laptops. No one answered. I
> felt so deflated that I lost energy and couldn't get my enthu-
> siasm back for the rest of the class.*

If he adopts a non-judgmental disposition towards the event,
that teacher might use the following six steps to explore it:

1. *Set the Stage:* Start by recalling, in detail, the lead-in to
   the session. Jot down notes to fix the moment in your
   mind. Remember the sights, sounds, smells, tastes,
   feelings of the moment. Who was present? How long
   was it? How was I feeling when the event started (prepared? preoccupied? hungry? excited? fearful?, etc.)

For this example: I remember rushing to class from a faculty committee meeting that had been quite tense. At the classroom door, I realized I had left some of my lecture notes in my office and didn't have time to go back and get them. Additionally, several students walked in late, and seveal were missing; they were first year students, and their first big memorandum of law school had been due that morning. I had skipped breakfast and was tired; I also hadn't slept well, and to compensate, had drunk more coffee than usual, so I felt a bit wired. The classroom, was hot and stuffy; we opened the windows and adjusted the thermostat, but that wasn't much help. The students yawned often during the class; now that I think of it, I did too. I was frazzled by the missing notes, and started haltingly, backtracking serveral of times.

2. ***Recall in Detail:*** Exactly what happened? Make a timeline of events from start to finish—no event is too small. Adopt the discipline of writing only facts—not conclusions or evaluations (e.g., not "they looked bored", but "they had no expressions on their face; they did not make eye contact with me; they were looking intently at something on their screens; they said nothing; they didn't nod; they were slumped in their chairs").

For this example: Because fewer students than usual were present, I waited several minutes before starting class. The students who were there opened their laptops and began surfing, or doing whatever else they were doing. I spent a moment posting my PowerPoint on our class online Blackboard and told those who were present where it was. Then we waited some more. Frankly, I was feeling discombobulated—wired, without my notes, hot, wondering where the missing students were.

When I finally started class, I felt a different person from the one who prepared it. When I made the slides, I was energized, and had a real sense that this was the answer to teaching this material; now I felt deflated, flat. Since I was feeling wired, in order to calm myself down, I was talking deliberately slower, and that may have seemed artificial. But when I got to the chart, for which I had no notes, I rushed through it, spending less than a minute on it; and when I got to the outline, I was also cursory. I remember saying several times—"we'll get to this next week." As I clicked to the third slide, I remember thinking, "This isn't going to work." Now that we were in class, it looked silly to me.

At that moment, I looked up at the students. I realize now that I hadn't looked at them much since I had started lecturing and showing the slides. To a person, they were looking at their laptops, with expressions I couldn't read. Some were typing; one was yawning. I asked if they had any questions, and no one even looked up. I could feel all the energy leaving my body. And there were forty minutes left to class!

3. **Identify Key Moments:** these simply may be the moments that stood out for you. Focus on a few turning points in the event.

There were two key moments: i) Moving from the chart to the outline (for which I did not have my notes); ii) Moving from the joke slide to looking up at the students faces and seeing blank stares.

4. **For Each Moment, Recall More Details:** What specific words were said? If there was silence, how long was it? What facial expressions appeared? How many people were actively involved? How much eye contact did the speakers share?

Moving from the chart to the outline (for which I did not have my notes): thinking back on it now, I remember not wanting to spend time on the chart, because I wasn't confident I could answer questions without my notes. I realize that I didn't ask for questions after the chart, which I usually do; I actually didn't want questions. Perhaps I conveyed

2 · REFLECTION

that. Maybe that's why I also rushed through the outline—I was just in a rushing mode.

What kind of language did I actually use? I framed the presentation in terms of what we would learn in the future. (Without those notes, I really didn't want to engage the complicated information.) No one else spoke—I didn't invite anyone to.

Even before I looked up at the students, I was sure the class was a bust, that I'd never be able to teach this material. I remember feeling sheepish when I looked up, embarrassed by my joke. But it didn't matter. The students didn't even get it. Maybe they weren't even listening.

What specifically were they doing? They were staring at their laptops. Their faces seemed expressionless. They did not speak.

5. *Articulate Your Interpretation of What Happened:*

   My lecture fell flat—the students didn't get it. All that work for nothing. This topic is just too difficult to teach. The next months of teaching this subject are going to be endless.

6. ***Brainstorm Alternative Explanations that Explain the Same Facts:*** Aim for 10 alternative explanations for each moment.

   1. *The students were exhausted (paper due that morning), and the hot, stuffy room didn't help.*

   2. *The students were preoccupied with something else (paper due that morning).*

   3. *The students were looking at the PowerPoint I created.*

   4. *The students were following, but were saving their questions, because they knew we'd discuss the materials over the next weeks.*

   5. *The students had questions, but because of the pace at which I was going, they didn't feel comfortable making me pause to ask them.*

   6. *The students were actively engaging the materials and had no questions.*

7. *The students were tuned out, and wouldn't have responded, no matter what I did.*

8. *The PowerPoint shut people down, and discouraged discussion.*

9. *The students were concerned and confused, because I wasn't acting like myself.*

10. *The students didn't understand that the last slide was a joke.*

Where the reflection goes from here is up to the reflector. The key shift made by the discipline of non-judgment is to push the reflector to move beyond his instant negative (or positive) judgments and to focus instead on details and facts. Too often we may base those judgments on insufficient information. In this way, non-judgment also may give us the courage to look at events that seem negative and unpleasant to learn from them without fear of constant harsh self-criticism.

Here are some additional components which many of our retreat colleagues have reported to be useful components for reflection; they also are useful in constructing and sustaining a process you can trust.

- Solitude or the company of an absolutely trustworthy companion;
- Sufficient time to enter a proactive state of thinking (minimum of 15 minutes);
- Entering reflection through a meditative process—running, praying, meditating, yoga—any repetitive process that engages the entire mind and moves one out of the previous rhythm and concerns.[7]

We'll return to these components in Section IV B. below, exploring how to create conditions conducive to reflection.

Take a moment to consider whether any of our recommendations provide ideas for your reflection. Feel free to incorporate parts or all of them or to reject parts or all of them. We hope to offer suggestions that may lead to useful ideas for your unique, idiosyncratic process.

III. A Session of Reflection: The Individual Reflection Event

In this section we focus on creating an individual session of reflection. At our retreats, we required each participant to design and execute what we called an "individual reflection event." Here we suggest how you might develop such an event, and we offer several extended examples of successful ones.

A. Individual Reflection Event: The Retreat Model

We'd like to encourage and help you to design an individual reflection event, tailored to meet your most pressing needs for reflection and feedback. While others may become involved in the event, ultimately, it is aimed to serve an audience of one, and should be closely tailored to meet your idiosyncratic needs. Individual events are crucial in helping you listen attentively to yourself and to others on an issue important to you, making creative use of the resources available to your reflection practice. Individual reflection events are also vital to your efforts to create time for reflecting on your teaching beyond a retreat into your daily life.

Why did we require an individual reflection event at our reflection retreats? In the midst of our daily teaching lives, we have the acute sense that there is no time for reflection, indeed, that our daily activities somehow preclude us from the reflection we crave. Despite our deep and abiding desire to process the rich experiences which comprise our teaching days, some of us feel we have not yet found ways to do that processing in our daily lives.

For those who yearn to reflect, but wonder how to do so, an individual reflection event allows you to experiment with new processes for reflection or to employ trusted processes that have fallen by the wayside. What you discover constructing such an event may allow you to carry the process over to the hurly-burly of your daily life. An individual reflection event can be a way to begin a practice of mindful reflection that we describe later in this chapter. Here is a template.

Search for critical incidents of reflection, both positive and negative. On the positive side, remember a time when you felt you debriefed or reflected fruitfully, and look at that event in some detail.

1. *How did it start?* How did you make the time? How did you make the space?

2. *What was the subject of your reflection?* Was it a specific event, or a series of events, or something else?

3. *What were the conditions?* Be very detailed here. Where did the reflection take place? What made you comfortable and open to reflection there? Was there food? Was there music? What was the climate like? Were you alone? If you were with someone, who was it, and what was it about them that encouraged reflection?

4. *What were the fruits of your reflection?* For example, did you keep a journal, write a letter to yourself, or email a friend? Did you come away with an insight or two?

5. *After the reflection, did you alter your teaching?* What, if any, concrete effect did it have on your work?

Similarly, consider in detail any salient, failed experiments at reflection. The same questions can apply. Your goal is to identify blocks to reflection, obstacles that have impeded you in the past, and may continue to impede you until identified.

An individual reflection event is another chance to employ processes you can trust or to try out some new ones. Again, the more individually tailored, idiosyncratic, fitted to your specifications, the better. If it works for you, that's all that matters.*

---

* At our most recent retreat, we noted the following resources available to our conferees. Consider what resources are available in your community, at your school, among your trusted peers and friends, and develop a similar list.

To assist each participant, the retreat has the following built-in resources available:

1. a small group to which the participant is assigned, which has reserved 25 minutes for the specific purpose of helping the participant in designing, carrying out, debriefing or otherwise supporting his/her event;

2 · REFLECTION   41

Here are some examples of possible individual reflection events:

a) walk on a local hiking trail, alone or with a companion, reflecting or conversing on a specific topic or event from your teaching, followed by journaling and a letter to yourself;

b) read Mary Rose O'Reilley's *Radical Presence*, and journal about its relevance to your teaching;

c) talk with a small group of trusted friends about a teaching event from the past year that was particularly rich or bothersome;

d) teach part or all of a sample class to a group convened to help you perform your Reflection Event;

e) for a clinical teacher, simulate a sample case supervision of an intern;

f) get advice about an ongoing teaching problem;

g) convene a separate small group to talk about common interest (for instance, at one retreat, we convened

---

2. other periods: the meal times, free times at the end of the day and in the evening, the two free afternoons (Conference Centre rooms may be available to us after hours for these purposes, if desired—check with Mark and Jean);

3. some photocopying capability (see Mark and Jean);

4. the "wish board," a bulletin board where requests for other resources or help from other retreat participants can be posted;

5. the retreat co-facilitators, Mark Weisberg and Jean Koh Peters, as well as other conferees, who can help with brainstorming about the event (they are available during the lunch hours in the dining hall);

6. Banff Centre facilities, including an indoor pool, Jacuzzi, steam room, gym, climbing gym;

7. lovely natural surroundings, including hiking in nature;

8. reference books on teaching for loan or sale;

9. the retreat materials, which contain prompts for reflecting and some readings aimed at a reflection event;

10. a willingness to try to meet other, unanticipated needs (see Mark and Jean and see if they can help).

groups to discuss spirituality and law, technology and law, diversity);

h) use one or more reflection prompts in this book, alone or with company;

i) do a small bit of writing during the retreat, and present it to a small group of your friends.

And here are several suggestions for designing your reflection event:

Go where the energy is, positive or even negative. If you think you "should" do X, but are dying to do Y, by all means, do Y.

Set aside a fixed time for the event, and exclude all other agenda from the time—turn off your cell phone, avoid interruptions, put away other paperwork. Keep your time focused on this inquiry alone.

If the idea of making the event a "mini-retreat," even if very short, is appealing, consider these suggestions. Jennifer Louden, author of *The Woman's Retreat Book*, suggests that every retreat consists of four parts:

Prepare: Set an intention for the Retreat

Withdraw: from Ordinary Life through Ceremony and by Creating a Container

Listen: in Sacred Space

Re-emerge: into Ordinary Space and Time[8]

Louden suggests that such a retreat can be accomplished over several days, or even in a matter of a half an hour.

Here is one possible way to structure a retreat-based individual reflection event:

1. *create a space*—creating some distance between the object of reflection and the reflection (this can just be a willed thing—for instance, meditating in the middle of the event—if you can travel mentally, you don't have to go anywhere physically). You can involve a friend or another person, either contemporaneously (coffee, a walk), in staggered time (a letter or email), or in imagination (a letter to your deceased favorite el-

2 · REFLECTION

ementary school teacher ...); you also can involve a group.

2. *remember*—gather data about the object of reflection, attending to detail, emotion, intuition. Gather the data in a spirit of non-judgment; everything is a fact. Self-condemnation is not allowed.

3. *engage the data*—examine your data with a creative eye. Make observations, draw conclusions, and look for patterns that might not be obvious in the heat of the moment.

4. *choose a follow-up plan*—even not having a plan is acceptable, as long as you've chosen it.

Examples: create a to do list, plan your next reflection, find reading material, consult a friend. Consider a letter/note to yourself (described in detail in Chapter 6).

5. *schedule the follow-up*—literally, make an entry in your calendar scheduling at least one date for your follow-up plan.

6. *exit the space*—conclude your reflection time in a deliberate way. Make a transition back to ordinary time and space.

If it's consistent with your other goals, pick a fun venue. Meet outside, hike while you talk, meet in the pool; feel invited to be offbeat in your environment.

Consider keeping a journal as part of the event, or as a reflection after the event. This will allow you to keep a partial record that may encourage you to continue your processing.

Consider telling a few friends that you are planning the event, and organize a preparatory event before or a debriefing event after (a coffee meeting, an early dinner after work, etc.) to get their support for the event.

Organize the event around an intention you can state in one sentence: e.g., I want to think about how to lead more fruitful class discussion, or I want ten new ideas for teaching about criminal

44   2 · REFLECTION

suppression motions. Before the event ends, return to the sentence and take stock. This will promote focus throughout the event.

In the final analysis, perhaps the most important aspect of an individual reflection event is granting oneself permission to reflect. For many of our retreat participants, once the commitment to reflect was made, the planning came naturally, from their deep well of desire to debrief and their stored up experiences to mine. The concept of an event crystallizes the commitment and launches the reflection practice, which, for many, may become a more regular practice of mindful reflection throughout their teaching lives.

B. Examples of Individual Reflection Events

Here are two examples of reflection events, as reported by two retreat participants. The first reports on the event and reflects on it later; the second was written during a reflection event spontaneously undertaken weeks after the retreat.

1. Reflection Event—With a Group, at Our Retreat[9]

About a month before the Institute for Law School Teaching's Reflecting on Our Teaching conference, I received an email sent to all participants asking the following:

"1. What dimensions of your teaching life do you hope to reflect upon usefully?

2. Which one looms largest?"

Having these questions in advance was helpful—and daunting. I had been wondering about the retreat ever since I had heard about the one held three years earlier. While the prospect of spending three days with thoughtful people in a beautiful mountain setting was incredibly attractive, it was also quite scary. I had never been on a formal retreat. What if it turned out that I wasn't, after all, thoughtful or deep? That I wasn't really suited for this work that I thought I loved? That I was revealed to be the shallow and narrow-minded instructor some of my colleagues and students seemed to think I was? In a retreat setting, it would be hard to hide.

The helpful part was having to answer the questions in writing, in advance. As someone who learns from writing, composing my answers helped me clarify my goals for the retreat. My first thought was that I wanted to reflect upon helping students become metacognitive—learn about their own learning—by reflecting and writing about it. I wanted students to become comfortable sharing their reflections with me and their classmates.

I also wanted to reflect upon how I could better connect with students—how to be so that they felt I was treating them with dignity and respect. That they believed I honored them for who they are as individuals, not just as law students. I also wanted to see if I could figure out a better way to work with students so that they felt both valued for who they were but also challenged—I wanted to find a way to balance setting high expectations and rigor with understanding, compassion and empathy.

Because I see myself as a coach for lawyers-in-training, I also wanted to think about how I could help students learn about the legal world and its many permutations. I wanted to do a better job helping them competently function as professionals in that world. But in doing so, I wanted them not to lose the sense of self, their voices or their values. I had not felt valued in law school; I wanted to try to reduce that feeling with my students.

Answering the first question was easier than the second. As I wrote in my responses, I felt that my reflection goals were related. Teaching students how to reflect upon their learning should also help them integrate their lives before, during, and after law school. I wasn't sure, however, about the value of my goals and how the hell I would work on them in my "individual reflection event."

We'd been given plenty of information and guidance about this reflection event, including examples of what we might do. The message was clear from all conference materials and Mark and Jean: this reflection event was for us and about us. But what exactly should I do? I hoped that something would hit me when I got to the retreat.

It didn't. Instead I found myself assigned to a small group with five others, two of whom I knew and greatly respected. The other three taught impressive subjects about which I knew nothing, and were undoubtedly much smarter than me. I was going to have this "reflection event" with them? Here was the problem. We spent lots of time during the initial sessions of the conference reading, writing and thinking about who we were as teachers. We were reminded of our need to be authentic. To listen and trust our own minds. This was great. I loved this stuff. But it is one thing to read, write and talk about the need to be authentic and another to be put in a position of revealing yourself to the intelligent and wonderful people in your small group, all of whom you are afraid of disappointing or embarrassing.

During their reflection events, other group members seemed to know exactly what to do with their individual 25 minute sessions. They posed interesting problems. Told fascinating stories. Asked thoughtful questions. Shared ideas. It was an honor to be a part of their events. I was learning tons. But participating also made me more anxious. Intellectually I knew that my reflection event was for me, and that I should not worry about what others thought; still, I couldn't shed my emotional need for external validation. Perhaps my event could just be having the group engage in solitary writing, with no discussion.

Imposing isolation on myself and not getting feedback from the group was not, however, truly what I wanted. I wanted the group's input. I valued and trusted these colleagues. They could really help me with something important. And Mark and Jean had charged us to make the retreat work for us individually. They had also asked us to be kind and loving towards ourselves. If I was going to do what I wanted—talk about teaching students to reflect upon their learning—I was going to need someone else to reassure me that was ok. I sought out external validation, feeling like a total loser. During a break, I casually chatted with two members of my group about my desire to do a better job teaching students the skill of metacognition. Did they think that was worthy of an individual reflection event? They did.

When it was my turn for the individual reflection event, I explained that I wanted to figure out a better way of teaching metacognition. I had long believed that reflecting—in writing—was an incredibly useful exercise. I knew that Olympic athletes reflected about their performances, as did other professionals. This self-awareness contributed to making great leaders. On a personal note, it had helped keep me sane through career changes, emotional crises and parenting two kids. Reflecting and writing allowed me to become clearer about what I was thinking and feeling.

Following my gut about the importance of reflecting in writing, in some years I had required students to write reflective essays about what they were learning. Not all, but plenty of the student evaluations were scathing. "Way too many touchy-feely assignments." "Professor makes us do pointless writing—big waste of time." Ashamed and dismayed, I had stopped including reflective writing in my courses. I wondered if I had been imposing something stupid on most students.

Two things had recently made me think that I wanted to reincorporate reflective writing exercises. One was the input from several upper level students. As one said, "You know, I hated those reflective papers you made us write last year, but now I realize that they were really helpful. You should require them again." The second was learning that there was a scientific basis for the value of reflecting. Termed "metacognition," reflecting upon one's learning was identified to be one of the four key components to learning across all ages and disciplines.

These events convinced me to re-introduce reflection in my courses, but how? How to avoid the wretched "T-F" (touchy-feely) comments? I believe that words have strong power. Was there a way to name these reflective writings so that students would be more receptive?

The group's responses were awesome. "Introduce it as science. The first time you do it, spend a few minutes explaining that this comes from decades of research. Give the students the reasons behind why you are requiring this."

"Use the fancy words. Call it metacognition. Makes it sound scientific."

"Ask for the students' forbearance. Explain that this works for you and many, many others, but that it might not click with them now. Ask for their patience. Other things will work for them."

"Call the reflective writing assignments something technical, such as 'problem-solving protocols' or 'cognitive protocols.' "

As someone who teaches writing, and constantly emphasizes the power of "Plain English," the notion of hiding behind jargon didn't sit well. But I suspected it would work.

In the two years since that retreat, I have done just what the wise members of my group recommended. I introduce the scientific grounds for writing about learning. For a few minutes, students are given an overview of metacognition, including an explanation about why they are going to be asked to engage in reflective writing about their learning during the course. Students receive sheets titled things like, "Cognitive Protocol—Memo 2." Not all students are convinced about the value of these exercises, but most are.

After I tried this new approach, I wanted to find out what the students' perceptions were. During the second semester of a year-long writing course I asked them if they understood why they were asked to spend time in class writing about what they had been learning. Most of them looked at me with the expression of "Du-u-u-h, of course we do." And then proceeded to discuss why it helped them to be pay attention to and write about their own learning. Their answers were perceptive and thoughtful. Perhaps they were just telling me what they thought I wanted to hear, but if so, they sounded remarkably like the text books' descriptions.

The 2003 retreat's reflective event extended beyond my classroom. I presented "Teaching Metacognition" twice at the Institute for Law School Teaching national teaching conferences, and was fortunate to then be invited to give similar workshops elsewhere. I'm in the process of working on an article about teaching metacognition. I am slowly learning to trust my own mind. It's possible that I would be doing this without the reflective event, but I doubt it. And even if I were, it wouldn't have happened as quickly. With the input of my group, the reflection event allowed me to improve the way I taught something I cared deeply about. It helped me develop confidence in sharing my teaching ideas with others. It has strengthened my resolve to continue to write about teaching.

2 · REFLECTION

Looking back, I think I know what made me so scared about the reflection event. It was its importance. It wasn't just a simple question about teaching technique, or looking ignorant in front of others. This reflection event was about wanting to be valued for doing something most students didn't like. Something that I thought was important, that I didn't want to give up. In retrospect, I was terrified that the group might tell me that I should give up the practice of having students write about their learning. If they had recommended that, and I had followed their suggestion, I would have felt a horrible loss. But if I rejected the suggestion, I would be forced to acknowledge that I was rigid and narrow-minded. That would have meant that teaching was, after all, about my agenda, and not the students' learning. That would expose me to truly be a fraud. And that was too painful to think about.

At the retreat two years ago, none of these fears were conscious. I just had the overwhelming sense of anxiety, made all the worse for not having its origin fully identified. One of the many gifts of the retreat was that I developed the strength to encounter those unarticulated fears. When I decided that I would use my reflection event to talk about teaching metacognition, I had hoped that the group would be supportive and give me a few good ideas. I knew from the previous time with the group that they would be at least that. I wasn't really hoping for anything more than that. That the group would not only think what I wanted to do was valuable but give me tools to do it much better was beyond my wildest dreams.

I'd love to report that I have continued to engage in the depth of reflection that I did during the retreat. I haven't. I write about my teaching and think about individual classes and ways to improve them, but I haven't considered the two questions Mark and Jean sent us: 1) What dimensions of your teaching life do you hope to reflect upon usefully? 2) Which one looms largest? Writing this, I realize what a gift it was to have thought about those questions and receive input from others. It inspires me to find a way to incorporate this kind of in-depth reflection into my life again soon.

2. Reflection Event—Alone, at a Conference, Further Reflected Upon Alone, after the Conference[10]

November 8, 2005
University of Western Ontario

Dear Mark,

It is just after 8 am and I am sitting in a corner at Windermere Manor on a spontaneous "guerilla retreat." On the drive into work I decided to carve out a bit of solitude and was drawn up the hill to this mansion-turned-conference center. I'm just working away here letting the staff assume that I'm some big shot preparing for an important meeting.

Here comes a fresh faced, uniformed young man now. Maybe he'll ask which group I'm with. Maybe he'll ask me to leave?

"Could I bring you a coffee, sir?"

"Well, actually, a Earl Grey tea, black, would be lovely, thank you."

The tea arrives shortly. I push my luck and ask for a croissant. Diana Krall is singing to me softly. Nice.

The first couple months of term have been hectic with the campus-wide implementation of the clicker project and ongoing renovations to our building that have displaced me from my office. In the midst of this disorienting situation, I've recently received my letter to myself from the Retreat as well as your email acknowledging the Globe and Mail coverage of my course. This correspondence has drawn my mind back to Banff. I'm recalling my intention to respond to your invitation for us to share our experiences on the Retreat.

My personal reflective event came upon me unexpectedly. I was journaling one evening around an exercise looking at a series of provocative quotes about teaching. Worries about what to do for my "event" were simmering in the back of my mind. The quote that had infected me that afternoon was from Parker Palmer and was related to the interface between the world's Deep Hunger and my Deep Gladness. I've just found the following passage in my journal from my writing that evening.

"the place where Gladness and the world's Deep Hunger meet. Yeah right. Just try to work on that edge without being consumed by the pit of need. Bitten off. Chewed. Soaked in acid and bile. All your juices extracted from husks shat into a pile. Only to be consumed all over again by some more primitive Hunger. Gladness cannot be sustained by the Hunger, only drained."

I guess I was feeling pretty depleted. But then the reflective event happened. There was a shift and my pen began to wonder …

"What if Deep Hunger is not a bottomless pit? What if Hunger is just a pole; one end of a continuum stretching out toward Deep Fulfillment on the horizon? What if it's all just about FLOW? What if I just need to conduct the flow from Deep Fulfillment to Deep Hunger? What if I stop trying to fill up the pit with bits of my own flesh? What if Gladness is the simply the experience of conducting energy?"

I know the word "transformative" is overused to the point of cliché but I don't hesitate to stamp it onto this page. My brief experience of shifting perspective changed the core metaphor that I use to understand how I am in the world. This, in turn, changes everything in ways that I really like.

I once thought that I had to go out into the world and accumulate knowledge, consume it in ways that would give me bulging, scholarly, muscles that defined me as a Teacher. I would then feed students who were Hungry and I derived some type of Gladness from this exercise. However, over the years, with thousands of students, I couldn't keep up. I ran out of scholarly morsels to go around and eventually began to give away my flesh and bones. Sadness.

I understand now that I got into this trouble by interrupting the flow. By trying to make knowledge my own so I could dress myself up in it in ways that everyone would recognize me as a teacher worthy of respect, I inserted my ego and blocked the flow. However, if knowledge belongs to everyone, and all I have to do is conduct it from a "source" to a "sink," well, this makes me smile from deep inside. This is how the frighteningly infinite sucking Hunger can be balanced—by infinite gushing Fulfillment.

So, my Job Description from the Retreat is simple. Conduct the Flow from the Gushing to the Sucking.

Like all conductors, I have some resistance that may cause me to eventually wear out, but I no longer feel like I'm being pecked to death. I may get weary, but now my fatigue is part of a cycle of renewal rather than the one-way street of depletion. The infinite Hunger is no longer frightening. In fact, if the Hunger were ever truly satisfied, then the flow would stop—bringing the end of the Gladness that I now thrive on.

Only four minutes of writing amid only four days of Retreat had a dramatically positive impact on my current well-being and hope for the future. For this I am grateful to you and Jean for your initiative in running the Retreat, to the other participants who helped to spin the atmosphere and to myself for having the good sense to go to Banff in the first place.

Oh, my croissant has arrived. "Thank you."

And it is warm.

'til next time ...

IV. What a Practice of Mindful Reflection Might Look Like

Once you have a clearer understanding of what a fruitful session of reflection looks like, based on your idiosyncratic needs and goals, you may decide you want to nurture a regular practice of reflection. Again, the structure and logistics of this practice may now be crystal clear, grounded in the ideas you've developed here. Nevertheless, if for some reason, developing a practice of reflection still seems too daunting or not yet possible to achieve, read on.

A. The Spirit of Mindful Reflection — A Practice, Not a Habit

We recommend that you aspire to, not only the *habit* of seeking reflection, but a habit of *practicing* reflection. As we will discuss below, habits, which tend to be "repetitive, automatic, involuntary, regular," are critical to developing a practice, as a busy

2 · REFLECTION

teacher makes a habit of setting aside time and creating the conditions for fruitful reflection. However, once a teacher successfully gets to reflection, she usually does not want to go through the motions of a refined, unconscious habit, but instead, wants to look afresh and with a beginner's mind at the experiences of her teaching life. Like a yoga student who needs to develop good habits to get to yoga class (putting her mat by the door, clearing her calendar, leaving home on time), but who, once in class, needs to pay full mindful attention to what she is doing, a reflecting teacher creates and uses habits to condition herself to put aside time and create space for reflection. But once she begins, she wants to put aside those routine dispositions in favor of a fully mindful disposition.

Developing a reflection practice requires a teacher to break the cycle of mindlessness and practice mindfulness, in times of quiet, of crisis, of top speed, or of sabbatical. Our goal is to provide a resource for gradually developing daily rhythms for regular reflection.

The leading American proponent of mindfulness and its practice, Jon Kabat-Zinn, defines mindfulness as "openhearted, moment-to-moment, non-judgmental awareness."[11] Regular mindfulness practices, such as meditation, yoga, and tai chi, cultivate the mind's ability to maintain an extremely high level of paying attention in the moment. Mindful listening incorporates the four major signature characteristics of mindfulness: 1) awareness, that is 2) openhearted, 3) centered in the present moment, and 4) non-judgmental.

Before we explore more about the relationship between mindfulness and reflection, we must note some apparent tensions between the two concepts. First, mindfulness deliberately prioritizes and prizes the present, *this* moment; reflection focuses on processing and mining the past. Second, mindfulness seeks non-judgment, whereas in reflection, teachers will often specifically seek to evaluate what they did and plan for how they want to proceed in the future.

Nevertheless, the tensions do not run deep. There is no contradiction when one seeks to reflect mindfully, aware of one's process and surroundings, about something that has happened in the past. In addition, as we discussed above, in reflection, teachers can fully employ attitudes of non-judgment while also developing useful ideas for future teaching. In fact, the spirit of non-judgment may provide one of the only ways for a teacher to be comfortable beginning the process of examining an event that was painful at the time, or that the teacher believes will show her in an unfavorable light.

Here's another way to think about whether the substance of reflection is a habit or a practice. In *The Empathic Communicator*,[12] William S. Howell describes a five-point scale of "coping with change," called "Levels of Competence." The five points can be applied to reflection as follows:

1. *Unconscious Incompetence*—At this stage a person may not be able to reflect fruitfully and may have no awareness that she can't. It may be that people in this state will decide that they have no need for reflection, or that their current modes of reflection suit them fine.

2. *Conscious Incompetence*—Here, a teacher may realize that he is unable to reflect, either because of inability to resolve the logistics of setting aside the time and creating the space, or because he doesn't know what to do when he gets to reflect, but is unaware of how to alter the cycle. Conscious incompetence is an uncomfortable place. And because it's uncomfortable, it's also unstable—in conscious incompetence a person is motivated by the discomfort to seek to move down (to denial and unconscious incompetence) or up (to learning and conscious competence).

3. *Conscious Competence*—Here, a reflector consciously attempts to learn and apply the steps to reflection, perhaps through careful design of a first individual reflection event. With conscious effort, she can begin to do so regularly.

4. *Unconscious Competence*—With time and experience, one can create habits and deeply etched understanding, so that making time for reflection, and reflecting, are automatic and ongoing.

5. *Unconscious Super-competence*—Here "the total resources of the human being achieve harmonious inte-

gration" as a teacher regularly benefits from peak experiences of spontaneous reflection.

Mindful reflection practice constantly focuses a reflecting teacher on stages 2 and 3. In some ways, one never wants to become confident or unconscious about reflection—the characteristics of observing things freshly, starting at the beginning, examining details from scratch, require the kind of awareness in mindful practices that Kabat-Zinn and others recommend. In fact, we come to reflection often precisely to combat the mindlessness of our daily life—the feeling that we are racing through our lives unconsciously, relying on habit and on the clock running out and deadlines passing rather than embracing each day as an important piece of a lifelong vocation. Like the professor who keeps walking to the door of an old office, now assigned to another, we get trapped in our habits when they are ingrained in us without relation to their current importance. It would be wonderful if a teacher could achieve unconscious competence in conquering the *logistics* that bar reflection; once the teacher gets to the reflective moment, however, let it be a fully aware, conscious, mindful time. Thus, the spirit of mindful reflection seeks mindfulness throughout the process—non-judgment, moment-to-moment awareness, openheartedness.

B. The Structure of Mindful Reflection— Useful Strategies

While there are an infinite number of ways to reflect, in this book we emphasize five major, and overlapping, modes of reflection:

1. *Reflecting on a text*—using excerpts from other teachers as a springboard for reflection.

2. *Reflecting on critical incidents in one's teaching*—focusing on identifying and examining specific moments in one's teaching life.

3. *Reflecting with one other, or in a group*—asking others to help you reflect.

4. *Reflecting in writing*—using journaling, freewriting, quick writes, letters to oneself to promote and memorialize reflection.

5. *Creating individual reflection events*—creating reflection to meet one's unique and idiosyncratic needs.

C. Additional Suggestions for Developing a Reflection Practice

Here are some ways to develop the (practice/habit) of reflection (tips/tools):

1. Downshifting, Making the Transition

Why do so many teachers yearn for time for reflection, and find themselves consistently foiled when they try to seek it? One central challenge can be summarized by the need for timeshifting, a concept illuminated by Dr. Stephan Rechtschaffen. Rechtschaffen recommends three steps to timeshifting:[13]

a.) "Become aware of the present"—he suggests using mindfulness practices including breath awareness, meditation, yoga and the like;

b.) "Sense the particular *rhythm and flow* of the moment"—what is the rhythm to which I am currently entrained?

c.) "Create time shifting rituals"—Rechtschaffen describes several—from taking a walk, to washing the dishes, to taking a shower after getting home from work. Rechtschaffen suggests that we distinguish habit from ritual by asking, "If I were consciously trying to change my rhythm, would I do this?" Rechtschaffen suggests that habits tend to reinforce a sameness of rhythm, while these rituals actually shift rhythm.[14] Rechtschaffen notes that rituals that can be easily incorporated into daily life tend to fall into one of six categories:

2 · REFLECTION

- *Being in the moment*
- *Creating time boundaries*
- *Honoring the mundane*
- *Creating spontaneous time*
- *Doing what we like to do*
- *Creating time retreats*[15]

2. Giving Oneself Permission

With such busy lives, with so much to do, our resistance to reflection can be powerful. It can help just to say *yes*, to give oneself permission to reflect.

3. Dealing with Technology and Time

Do laptops, Dictaphones, and iPods assist or detract from your entry into reflective space? If it's the latter, consider changing your regular routine to pave the way into reflection. If you're tied to a screen, would writing in a journal or on a pad of paper change your rhythm? If you rely on the written word, would dictating into a recorder offer you a different avenue for expression?

D. Creating Conditions for Reflection

Consider:

1. Escaping—the need to disengage, to get distance to see clearly
2. Being in a safe space, or with safe people
3. Seeking beauty: e.g., time in nature
4. Having fun

Reflection can be great fun. Counterposed to a life of ongoing tasks and challenges, the respite of solitary or communal reflection on a teaching life will offer a welcome change, and that change can be structured to be enjoyable as well as nourishing.

At one of our retreats, Jean was choosing between two topics for her reflection event: 1) how she reacts to negative evaluations of her teaching and 2) how to develop a play ethic that rivals her work ethic. She decided to set up an event focusing on topic 1 that included her own journaling, talking with a close trusted friend, and reading some evaluations from the semester just past. After the event, she found that while it had been extremely fruitful, doing it had felt quite heavy. That made her wonder why she had abandoned topic 2. As a lark, in her journal the next day, she brainstormed ten kooky, playful things that she could do with negative evaluations:

1. roll each into a ball and play ping pong with it.

2. read evaluations in a yarn store or toy store.

3. read the evaluations while mini golfing.

4. read your evaluations in the pool.

5. use a sparkler to light a particularly annoying one on fire.

6. imagine what Captain Picard[16] would do.

7. sing the evaluations: Wagner for the negative ones, Up with People for the positive ones.

8. play rhythm instruments as you read each one.

9. imagine tangoing with each person who wrote an evaluation and having a great time.

10. write a round about the toughest part of hearing the negative feedback.

During their prep time for the next day of retreat, she read them to Mark. Mark suggested that she read them to the group, as another possible element of a reflection event. As we talked, we had the idea of turning the reading into a game—"Can you top this?" Jean eventually read the list to the group, asking the group, for each one, to come up with a related item that was even more absurd. Maybe you can come up with your own.

V. Conclusion

In this chapter we've described what we mean by reflection and why we think it's an important dimension of a teacher's life, as well as offering you several suggestions for beginning or sustaining your own practice. In the following chapter, we focus on one often-overlooked practice related to reflection: listening.

60 2 · REFLECTION

Notes

1. Suzanne Goldsmith suggests that reflection should be continuous, noting that "reflection should be a habitual activity, an ongoing conversation with the self (although conversation may, at times, include others) that moves hand in hand with the experience." *Journal Reflection: A Resource Guide for Community Service Leaders and Educators Engaged in Service Learning* (Washington: American Alliance for Rights and Responsibilities, 1995), 2.

2. Wayne Muller, *Sabbath: Finding Rest, Renewal, and Delight in Our Busy Lives* (New York: Bantam, 2000), 70.

3. For instance, the morning pages in Julia Cameron's *The Artist's Way: A Spiritual Path to Higher Creativity* (New York: Tarcher/Putnam, 1992), 9.

4. Jean Koh Peters and Susan Bryant, "The Five Habits for Cross-Cultural Lawyering" in *Race, Culture, Psychology, and Law*, eds. Kimberly Hold Barrett and William H. George (Thousand Oaks, CA: Sage Publications, Inc., 2005); Susan Bryant, "The Five Habits: Building Cross-Cultural Competence in Lawyers," *Clinical Law Review* 8 (2001): 33–107; and Jean Koh Peters, "Representing the Child-in-Context: Five Habits of Cross-Cultural Lawyering," in *Representing Children in Child Protective Proceedings: Ethical and Practical Dimensions*, 3d Ed. (Charlottesville: LexisNexis, 2007).

5. Jon Kabat-Zinn, *Full Catastrophe Living: Using the Wisdom of Your Body and Mind to Face Stress, Pain, and Illness* (New York: Delta, 1990), 33.

6. Jalal al-Din Rumi, *The Essential Rumi*, trans. Coleman Barks with John Moyne (New York: Harper Collins, 1995), 36. The remainder of the poem reads:

When the soul lies down in the grass,
the world is too full to talk about
Ideas, language, even the phrase *each other*
doesn't make any sense.

7. Stephan Rechtschaffen, *Timeshifting: Creating More Time to Enjoy Your Life* (New York: Doubleday, 1996), 21 et seq.

8. Jenifer Louden, *The Women's Retreat Book* (San Francisco: Harper San Francisco, 2004), 27–29.

9. Sophie Sparrow of Franklin Pierce Law School provided this response during the retreat. It is reprinted here with her permission.

10. Tom Haffie provided this response by letter following the retreat. It is included here with his permission.

11. Jon Kabat-Zinn, *Coming to Our Senses: Healing Ourselves and the World Through Mindfulness* (New York: Hyperion, 2005), 24.

12. William S. Howell, *The Empathic Communicator* (Long Grove: Waveland Press, 1986).

13. Rechtschaffen, *Timeshifting*, 76–83.

14. Ibid., 80–81.

15. Ibid., 83.

16. *Star Trek: The Next Generation* (TV Series). One playful participant suggested that Jean change this to "What would Lieutenant Worf do?" transforming the question to involve a warrior perspective rather than a diplomatic captain's perspective.

Chapter 3

Experiments in Listening[*]

Attention: deep listening. People are dying in spirit for lack of it. In academic culture most listening is critical listening. We tend to pay attention only long enough to develop a counterargument; we critique the student's or the colleague's ideas; we mentally grade and pigeonhole each other. In society at large, people often listen with an agenda, to sell or petition or seduce. Seldom is there a deep, open-hearted, unjudging reception of the other. And so we all talk louder and more stridently and with a terrible desperation. By contrast, if someone truly listens to me, my spirit begins to expand.

—*Mary Rose O'Reilley,*
Radical Presence[1]

Critical listening. An integral part of critical thinking. An essential component of academic life. What we expect from ourselves, and what we hope to encourage in our students. Bred in our bones.

Yet it's not the only form of listening. And it may not always be the most useful form. Consistently listening with our critic mind can be bad for the listener, possibly worse for the one to whom we're listening. If we're too busy formulating our responses, we may miss what our interlocutor is saying. And we may put our interlocutor on the defensive; worse, feeling judged, she may shut down entirely, become dispirited, learn nothing. That's certainly

---

[*] A version of this chapter was published in *The Journal of Legal Education* 57 (2007): 427–47.

not what we want for our students, nor is it what we want for ourselves.

If the quality of our listening can affect how and what our students learn and can affect our interpersonal relationships, including those with our colleagues, we think that as teachers and clinicians, we can benefit significantly from exploring how we listen in our academic and professional lives. This is especially true, because we spend so much of our academic, professional, and personal lives listening or being listened to. As one commentator has reported, "[r]esearch demonstrates that 70 percent of our waking time is spent participating in some form of communication. Of that time, 11 percent is spent writing, 15 percent reading, 32 percent talking, and 42 to 57 percent listening."[2] But as she also notes, although listening may be "the type of communication we engage in the most and learn first, it requires a skill we are taught the least."[3]

How *do* we listen in our classrooms and with our colleagues? In those contexts are we consistently judgmental, always in our critic mind? Does that cause some of our students, even some of our colleagues, to shut down, to be unable to learn effectively?[4] Experiencing us as judgmental, will our students adopt that model, and if so, will it make them less effective in their professional lives? If we're not always listening in our critic mind, how else do we listen, and how does that affect our students and colleagues? More generally, what is the relationship between how we listen or are listened to and how we and others learn?

In this chapter we'd like to explore these questions with you, to invite you to reflect on your extensive experiences of listening, and to look with fresh eyes at how you might use those experiences to improve how you listen and are listened to. We think doing so will make us more effective teachers and learners.

We argue that a skillful listener will not be simply a critical listener, but will have available a variety of listening modes, and in any setting, will carefully choose which mode is appropriate for that setting. She will use a wide repertoire of skills and make subtle, sophisticated choices about listening in each new context; at any moment, she will be conscious of distractions and obstacles

3 · EXPERIMENTS IN LISTENING

and will strategize to eliminate impediments to optimal listening. To explore what those modes might be and how we might use them to facilitate learning and effective teaching is our goal.

To help us achieve that goal, we've included four sets of exercises, designed to appeal to differing styles of learning. Each takes its own unique form. Some are prompts for reflecting that invite quick brainstorming or fast, exploratory freewriting; we hope these will help you access the tacit knowledge that lies under the surface of your consciousness.[5] Other exercises are more analytical and ask for sustained attention. So while one exercise might work for you, another might not. As you read, feel free to work with those exercises that seem particularly interesting, challenging, or intriguing. Whatever exercises you choose, we hope that working with them might lead you to reflect on the following ten questions about listening.

1. What is the role of listening in your teaching? What is the balance of listening and speaking in your work life? In your life as a whole?

2. What are the different ways in which you listen? Do you listen differently in your professional life than in other environments? Do you listen differently at work than you do at home?

3. When listening is called for, what would you describe as essential characteristics of high quality listening? How do you know when it's occurred?

4. Do you tend to listen skeptically or receptively? Do you find yourself typically wanting to refute what you hear or to support what you hear? Do you interrupt? When that happens, what's going through your mind?

5. How often do you listen with hopes of transforming the speaker or her experience by the end of the conversation? How much is your listening designed to inspire change?

6. How often do you have enough time to think between listening and responding? Do you regularly need more time than you feel is available?

66   3 · EXPERIMENTS IN LISTENING

7. What concrete circumstances or factors enhance your listening? By contrast, what concrete circumstances or factors detract from your listening?

8. Do you think that when listening, you're performing a message? For example, if you regularly give advice when you listen, does doing so tend to perform the message that people who come to you need help? Correspondingly, do you find yourself trying to prove something with your listening? In the way you listen and respond, do you ever find yourself trying to make gestures about your own identity? Is the advice-giver one who wants to be known as a helper? Does the active listener want to be known as caring? The doubter as a critical thinker?

9. What are your usual experiences as a person in being listened to? In general, do you feel that the people around you listen to you well? Is this consistent across work and personal lines? If you do not feel that people usually listen to you well, what specifically would you change, if you could?

10. What would change if everyone at work or home listened slightly better? As a person being listened to, what would you most want from your interlocutors?

_____

In the rest of this chapter we offer you four modes for exploring your experiences of listening. Our goal is to help each of you identify your unique concerns and goals for your listening and to offer strategies for achieving those goals, as well as to help you become more aware of how you listen, the choices you're making in your listening, and whether you want to change any of your current practices.

Two of our exploratory modes are retrospective, two prospective. The first retrospective method offers a series of exercises designed to ask analytical, left-brain questions about how you listen. These exercises attempt to pluck off of the top of your consciousness what your interests and concerns about listening are as you already understand them. The second, more right-brain, retrospective technique offers you a series of exercises to explore critical incidents from your past which may yield rich material to understand yourself better as a listener. These require you to look in depth at moments in your listening life that stand out as important over time and to try to look at them from several differing perspectives. Identifying your listening patterns and proclivities and comparing them to the range of possible listening styles, will allow you to gauge whether your current patterns are consistently optimal in your teaching and professional lives.

In addition to these two retrospective ways, we offer two prospective ways to think about your listening. The first prospective series of exercises focuses on how to collect new information about listening in your daily life; examples include keeping a listening log and examining how you listen on a particular day. Finally, the second prospective series of exercises invites experiments in listening. Consciously altering your patterns and habits of listening can contribute to this process in two ways: first, by creating new and slightly different experiences from which to analyze your values and goals in listening, and second, by offering you listening practices to achieve those goals that may be new to you. Taken together, we hope that these varied approaches offer you several different perspectives for taking a fresh look at something you have done every day of your life.

I. Looking Retrospectively at Your Experiences of Listening

This section offers several strategies to start exploring your extensive storehouse of listening experiences. Part A offers analytical or general questions about your listening as a whole. Part B suggests that you identify specific critical incidents from your own experience, and analyze them in depth.

68   3 · EXPERIMENTS IN LISTENING

A. Ask Analytical or General Questions about Your Listening

See if any of these questions offer a promising starting point for your reflection on your listening experiences.

1. Ten Freewriting/Brainstorming Prompts

The following prompts are designed as jumping-off points for free writing or journaling, but can also be used for non-written reflection. We particularly recommend freewriting, because it allows you to memorialize your reflection process, which may be useful as you continue to reflect on your listening over time.

1. *Think about why this chapter has caught your attention.* Journal about that.[6] Journal about the associations you make with the topic.

2. *How would you rate yourself as a listener, on a 1–10 scale?* As you begin this inquiry, how would you evaluate yourself as a listener? Write down the characteristics that you value most about a listener. Then rate yourself on each of these characteristics.

3. *When do you enjoy listening?* Check all that apply. Add additional settings that are important to you.

   I like:

   a. Being read to—as a child? as an adult?

   b. Hearing a story

   c. Hearing lectures

   d. Listening to books on tape

   e. Hearing the news on the radio

   f. Listening to students in class

   g. Listening to students in meetings in your office

   h. Listening to colleagues

   i. Listening to family members

   j. Other—list them

3 · EXPERIMENTS IN LISTENING   69

4. *How important is it to you to converse with good listeners? How often do you do that?*

5. *Who taught you how to listen?* When did that happen? Have your listening habits changed since then?

6. *What is the balance in your life between listening and talking, input and output?* as a teacher? as a colleague? as a spouse? a parent? a friend?

7. *Answer this question ten times:* I would be a better listener if _____.

8. *Look at the ten questions in the introduction to this chapter.* Attempt to answer any or all of the questions directly. Don't worry about partial answers. Use these answers as a starting point for your analysis. Flag any questions that particularly trouble or intrigue you. You may decide to return to them later.

9. *Brainstorm about the kinds of non-academic listening that you find yourself doing during the day.* Note those that contrast sharply with others. For instance, listening to the waitress give the specials at dinner for some people commands high-intensity attention for a short period. By contrast, listening or being available to a teenage child may require a long period in which a person is accessible and relaxed, but not forcing interaction. Brainstorm about as many kinds of listening as you find yourself doing during the day. How do you listen when the radio is on in the background in an office? How do you listen to conversations overheard at the bank? How do you listen to colleague at the faculty mailboxes? Brainstorm as many different contexts of listening as possible without analyzing any of them.

10. *Do the same for your academic and professional life.* Are there multiple levels of listening at work? How many different kinds of listening do you engage in during your work day? Are your listening styles more varied at work or outside of work?

2. *Explore Your Listening on a Doubting and Believing Spectrum*

One helpful way to examine one's listening employs a doubting and believing spectrum derived from an essay by Peter Elbow.[7] Elbow proposes that "we can improve our understanding of careful thinking or reasoned inquiry (and therefore improve our practice) if we see it as involving two central ingredients: what I am calling methodological doubt and methodological belief."[8]

Elbow suggests, rightly, that academic culture is primarily a doubting culture. We pride ourselves on our ability to criticize an argument, and we want our students to develop that skill. He argues that with our intellectual roots located in Socratic argument and Cartesian skepticism, it's not surprising that we understand careful thinking as equivalent to critical thinking, that we privilege challenging a claim over "the ability to enter into it and temporarily assent."[9] And as Elbow also suggests, "[our] emphasis on learning to be critical helps explain the tendency toward critical warfare in the intellectual and academic world—the fact that intellectuals often find it surprisingly difficult simply to hear and understand positions they disagree with."[10]

Ironically, as this passage indicates, rather than helping us develop our thinking, doubting often "caters too comfortably to our natural impulse to protect and retain the views we already hold." We know this from debates; how often does a debate or ferocious argument lead to new insights or lead anyone to change their mind?

Yet we need new insights, want to be open to differing perspectives, think that becoming educated means making up and changing our minds. For that, Elbow argues, we also* need methodological belief: "the ... systematic, disciplined, and conscious attempt to *believe* everything, no matter how unlikely or re-

---

* Since doubting is such a fixture in academic culture, like Elbow, we're focusing here on believing. But also like Elbow, for effective listening, we think we need both. As we suggest, which mode we use will be context dependent.

3 · EXPERIMENTS IN LISTENING 71

pellent it might seem—to find virtues or strengths we might otherwise miss."[11] It is a process in which "we are not trying to construct or defend an argument, but rather to transmit an experience or enlarge a vision."[12] Methodological belief "force(s) us genuinely to enter into unfamiliar or threatening ideas instead of just arguing against them without experiencing them or feeling their force. It thus carries us *further* in our developmental journey away from mere credulity."[13] Rather than encourage us to accept unquestioningly, to embrace false beliefs, believing helps us examine our beliefs and consequently, become better able to assess what knowledge is trustworthy. As Elbow puts it, "A belief is a lens and one of the best ways to test it is to look through it."[14]

This experiment in listening proposes to adopt Elbow's poles of methodological doubt and methodological belief as a spectrum that we call the doubting/believing spectrum. The spectrum works on two levels. One is as an analytical tool through which you can examine a critical incident of listening.* For example, if looking at an experience of listening, you found that you listened with Elbow's components of methodological belief, "the disciplined procedure of not just listening but actually trying to believe any view or hypothesis that any participant wants to advance,"[15] you would situate yourself at the believing end of the spectrum. Looking retrospectively, a reflective listener would decide he was at or near pure belief when he concludes that when he listened, he tended to take everything related by the speaker as true, and without challenging the speaker, sincerely tried to pursue the conversation as if everything were completely true.

On the other end of the spectrum, a reflective listener looking at a critical incident of listening would conclude that she listened with pure doubt if she questioned every statement, every assumption, every inference, every implication of the speaker's words. If we conclude after looking at a previous incident of listening that we did so solely intending to refute, to reconstruct, to contradict, we will have found ourselves on the side of pure doubt.

---

* The second level involves making doubting and believing into a game. See Section II B (a).

72   3 · EXPERIMENTS IN LISTENING

Here are some examples of pure belief, suggested by students and teachers. You can supply others from your own experience.

- sympathetic conversations with a grandparent
- listening on a crisis hotline
- listening by a therapist
- early lawyer-client or doctor-patient interviews
- a student attempting to learn a brand new theory or material from a teacher
- a friend listening to another friend in a time of utter distress
- listening to an expert consultant like an accountant, financial planner, etc.

And examples of pure doubt:

- law teaching through the Socratic method
- teachers listening to colleagues at a workshop on a paper in progress
- listening to a politician you do not trust
- listening to someone with a credibility problem
- arguing the negative side in a debate tournament
- when a friend comes and asks you specifically to be a reality tester and asks you to find everything wrong with something they're thinking or have written
- cross-examining a witness who is doing you harm

For this exercise, think about a few specific past experiences of listening, and for each one, try to locate yourself on the doubting and believing spectrum. It may be helpful to add this analysis to the next exercise.

B. Explore Critical Incidents from the Past

1. *High Points and Low Points as a Listener*[16]

Identify a time when you felt you listened to someone in a way that precisely matched what was needed in the circumstances, a time when you felt you were a "good" listener. Journal about the incident for five minutes. Invite detail: what were the moments in

3 · EXPERIMENTS IN LISTENING

the listening that stood out; what were the feelings you had that confirmed your sense that the enterprise had been successful; what reactions did you receive that led you to believe that this was a successful experience of listening?

Pick another occasion when you were disappointed in your listening: A moment when you might have told yourself, "I need to be a better listener." Observe the experience and describe it. Be aware of judgments you make about yourself as you describe the experience. Again observe the feelings, the feedback, the moments in the conversation that remain with you.

After you have journaled about them, compare the two experiences, alone or with a friend. Try to identify what's common to them. Identify how they differ. What do they tell you about the strengths and weaknesses of your listening?

2. *Profile of the Three Best Listeners I Know*

Identify three people on whom you regularly rely to listen well to you, or three people in your life or in your past who you identify as good listeners. Take time to describe each one in detail. For now, focus on describing, not on identifying themes. Try to be as detailed or nuanced as possible.

3. *High Points and Low Points as a Person Being Listened To*

Describe a time when you did not feel listened to. Describe a time when you were trying to say something, and it was not heard or was misheard in way that was important to you. Describe the experience in detail. Note the emotions that come up, and also observe and describe those.

Now describe a moment when you felt listened to. Again, describe the context, describe the person, describe the setting. Describe all the details that come to you. If feelings arise, also observe and describe them.

Alone or in conversation with another, search for common and contrasting themes in your two experiences; brainstorm about what you sought in those situations as a person who needed to be

74   3 · EXPERIMENTS IN LISTENING

listened to deeply. What did you want from your listener? What kind of listening? What characteristics? What affect?

II. Looking Prospectively: Analyzing Your Listening for New Insights

These second two sets of exercises focus on using your current and future experiences of listening as new data in the process of trying to understand better your goals for listening, and in light of those goals, to refine how you listen. The first set focuses on developing effective techniques for collecting data and looking at your current behavior; the second focuses on experiments you can conduct to help you alter your listening patterns over time.

The following exercises are examples of changes in listening behavior that a teacher could experiment with on any day, in any conversation, for any time.* At the end of the chapter, we've described an activity that incorporates many of these experiments in listening into a one-hour exercise that can be performed with a group. While these exercises offer examples of prompts that some people have found helpful for generating new ideas about their listening, they are the tip of the iceberg. We hope that you will be naturally drawn to design exercises that work well for you. All the exercises share one function: to focus our awareness on behaviors that we often undertake unconsciously, and to encourage us to attempt consciously to shift the dynamics in those behaviors.

A. Collect New Data

Some reflective teachers may find it useful to start developing habits for regularly collecting new data about their listening. Ini-

---

* For an example of one teacher's change in listening behavior, see Mark Weisberg, "Discerning the Gift," *Change: The Magazine for Higher Learning* 31, no. 3 (1999), reproduced in part in *Learning from Change: Landmarks in Teaching and Learning from Change Magazine 1966–1999*, ed. Deborah DeZure (Sterling: Stylus, 2000), 392–94.

3 · EXPERIMENTS IN LISTENING 75

tially, it can be challenging to figure out how to observe a behavior like listening, which we do constantly, and often unconsciously. Indeed, the idea of these exercises is to increase awareness of listening at the time, or close to the time, when it happens, and to record what actually happens.

How each of us collects data should connect to our long established daily habits. Those who keep daily calendars may wish to jot notes there; those who use smartphones might wish to add electronic notes to calendar items for meetings. Those who regularly journal could write notes in those journals. One could carry around a Post-it or memo pad for this purpose. A portable Dictaphone or a recording application on your smartphone might be helpful for those who prefer to record their observations orally.

However you keep your data, here are four suggestions for the kind of data to collect.

1. *Keep a Listening Log*—record as you go throughout the day.

2. *Observe your listening during an 8-hour day*—identify a propitious workday for paying close attention to the listening you do, and make a plan for recording your observations.

3. *Observe yourself listening for a 24-hour period*—identify a propitious day with work and non-work listening planned, and make a plan for recording your observations.

4. *Review the week—note key points of listening in the days just past*—identify a week for paying attention to your listening, and set a time (a half hour or so) for reviewing the week with a special eye for listening. Look for trends, critical incidents, rich moments, moments of intensity in your listening, and think about them again.

Here is one example of an insight in listening practice and the changes that resulted from a planned observation of one's listening patterns. Early in writing this piece, Jean observed her listening over a week, and had one major insight. She found that when listening to stories, descriptions of events, or other presentations

76   3 · EXPERIMENTS IN LISTENING

of ideas, she often experienced a "listening gap" after about two or three minutes. The gap began when something her interlocutor said sparked an idea or reminded her of something, and her mind would follow that idea for about 30 seconds to a minute, until she realized that she had lost the speaker's thread. When she returned to listening, she was concerned that she had missed key data or concerns, and found herself trying to reconstruct what she had missed, without having to ask the speaker to repeat it. This reconstruction effort detracted from her renewed listening.

After noticing this trend, Jean decided to change three things about her listening. First, as a conversation begins, she often informs students, colleagues, and other frequent interlocutors with whom she works closely about the gap, and asks them to be patient with her and to understand that her requests to repeat what they have just said has to do with her lapse, and not the clarity of their speech. Second, she now tries conscious ways to stay listening, paying specific attention at the two or three minute mark, keeping eye contact with her interlocutors, avoiding other distractions (turning away from the computer, turning off the ringer of the phone, removing papers relating to other concerns from her desk during the meeting). Third, with people whom she does not regularly work, she has developed a habit of asking for the repetition and apologizing for the gap, rather than trying to hide the lapse.

B. Experiment with Your Listening

1. Use the Doubting-Believing Spectrum: Two Variants

a. Play the Doubting/Believing Game

Prospectively, you can make doubting and believing into a game. A serious game, in which the two extreme positions become methodological: "artificial systematic and disciplined uses of the mind."[17] After looking at critical incidents of his doubting and believing, a reflective teacher may wish to play some version of this game. If a teacher concludes that he has been overly skeptical or tends in certain contexts to be more doubting than he wishes, or

3 · EXPERIMENTS IN LISTENING   77

that his students regularly respond to each other skeptically as doubters, the teacher can consciously experiment with the believing game: taking to be true everything that he and the class hears from someone proposing a thesis or an interpretation, and encouraging the ideas that student proposes to be expanded and taken to their logical conclusions. Similarly, the teacher can expand the believing game to encompass everything said by anyone during a discussion. By contrast, a teacher who decides that she and/or her class has been overly supportive of ideas that needed stricter scrutiny, can decide to play the doubting game with ideas they feel have been insufficiently probed.

The key to prospectively applying the doubting and believing spectrum is making conscious choices about how to listen: as a doubter? as a believer? You can make these choices in a classroom for (or with) a group of students, and you can make them in any conversation at any time, based on what whomever is speaking needs at that time. For instance, imagine at a faculty seminar asking a person presenting a paper whether she would like her audience to listen to her in a doubting or believing spirit. How would each of those strategies affect the texture and dynamic of the discussion? We know that early in her writing process, a writer may decide she needs the nurture and comfort of a creative, brainstorming, and hence, believing, audience.* However, near the end of that process, when a writer is closer to submitting her piece for publication, she may decide she wants it scrutinized by a rigorously strict and skeptical doubting crowd. That diverse set of needs also might be true for students trying to work out their position on an issue or solve a perplexing problem. That suggests that in working with or responding to writers or thinkers, we have to be active at both ends of the doubting/believing spectrum. Conse-

---

* [M]uch bad writing comes from trying to write to doubters—trying to blow a trumpet to an audience of lemon-suckers. The writer writes nervously, defensively, continually trying to fend off objections, and as a result her writing is often tangled. The main ideas are characteristically muffled and insulated.
Elbow, *Embracing Contraries*, 287.

78   3 · EXPERIMENTS IN LISTENING

quently, to help us become more flexible in adjusting to what our
students and interlocutors might need, it would be useful for each
of us to reflect on whether our conversations at work typically tend
to land us on one end of the spectrum, and then to experiment
with conversations that work from the opposite end.

While Elbow thinks academic life is heavily focused on doubting and consequently, emphasizes how much we need believing,
he also stresses that to be complete thinkers and writers, for our
thinking to be trustworthy, we need both doubting and believing.
He recommends that each of us aim for balance between them.
And he stresses that we should understand doubting and believing as processes that are "methodological: artificial, systematic, and
disciplined uses of the mind. As methods they help us see what we
would miss if we only used our minds naturally or spontaneously."[18]

The doubting and believing spectrum can be useful to listening
in a clinical legal context, when new law students and supervisors
discuss approaches to client interviewing. For instance, early in a
clinical experience, when a law student may have very little experience with clients, students often look for advice about how to
conduct their early interviews. One piece of advice Jean regularly
offers her students is to approach their clients in their initial interviews in a believing mode. Initial interviews alternate between
gathering facts and building rapport; playing the believing game
allows a new lawyer to establish rapport, to take seriously her
client's felt and presented views, and before asking critical or clar-
ifying questions, to hear and understand as a whole a client's story
and his perspective as he has seen fit to present it.

However, as their relationship progresses, it would be inappropriate for a lawyer to maintain a purely believing mode in her listening. As she begins to amass extrinsic evidence, which may contradict or make her skeptical about her client's position, the lawyer
and her client must collaborate, and the client must be confronted
with concerns about his case. In addition, the client must be prepared for skeptical adversaries, skeptical fact-finders and decision-
makers, and the range of doubt they will encounter throughout.
In fact, we would expect that a lawyer who failed to make her client

3 · EXPERIMENTS IN LISTENING 79

aware of the doubting to come while exercising only pure belief would have neglected an important dimension of her job.

Consequently, as a clinical teacher, Jean suggests to her students that as they listen to their client and prepare her for the presentation of her case, they regularly think about the balance between doubting and believing that they have exercised in their interactions with that client, and at any point in any interview decide consciously where they want to situate themselves on the doubting and believing spectrum. If a student or lawyer also has looked at critical incidents from his past, he may conclude that as a default, he feels much more comfortable when he has situated his listening at particular places on the doubting and believing spectrum. This will remind him to make sure that he spends time with the client on the parts of the spectrum that do not necessarily come naturally to him. For instance, Jean, who notes that she naturally tends to the believing end of the spectrum with clients and students, regularly engages in methodological doubt, with the client's agreement and participation, by offering moots and simulated administrative interviews and cross-examinations, so that the client can experience for herself the kind of doubt and skepticism she might face before a judge or administrative officer. In general, she encourages law students beginning practice to make sure they balance their belief and doubt with clients over the course of the law student/client relationship.

b. Try a Line-up

Line-ups encourage people to commit to a position and to do it with their bodies. They're particularly effective when working with a controversial topic, say, a story that raises questions about a lawyer's professionalism, or a complicated legal case with good arguments on either side, or with any question or problem on which opinions or experiences are likely to differ across a broad spectrum. They can be used on their own, at the beginning or end of a discussion, but Mark has found them even more useful when combined with an exercise he calls "3 minutes each way." Here's an example.

80   3 · EXPERIMENTS IN LISTENING

Let's say a class is discussing a story such as Louis Auchincloss's "Equitable Awards."[19] The family lawyer in that story is likely to seem highly professional to some, extremely unprofessional to others. The teacher will have placed a long strip of masking tape in a line on the floor, identifying one end as "professional" and the other end as "unprofessional." He then asks people to find their place on that line that represents their position on whether that lawyer is professional or unprofessional. After people find their places on the line, he invites everyone to find someone standing at a different place from them. Each person, in turn, has 3 minutes to tell his interlocutor why he's chosen his particular spot. The listener's job is just that: to listen. No interrupting, no challenging, no criticizing and, on the other hand, no affirming, no nodding: just listening. In a particularly apt and provocative phrase, Mary Rose O'Reilley calls this "listening like a cow."*

After 3 minutes and a prompt from the teacher, the pairs switch roles. If there's time after that, the teacher might invite comments from the participants about the experience: what they learned, how it felt.

What makes line-ups educationally useful? Just having people move and express their commitment physically can be a powerful experience, and for most people it's fun. Like writing, physically expressing an opinion commits you to it more strongly than simply thinking it; when people are committed to a position, they're much more likely to be engaged when they discuss it. The whole

---

* "What I'm trying to construct here is a theory of attention that depends little on therapeutic skill and formal training: listening like a cow. Those of us who grew up in the country know that cows are good listeners.... Cows cock their big brown eyes and twitch their ears when you talk. This is a great antidote to the critical listening that goes on in academia, where we listen for the mistake, the flaw in the argument. Cows, by contrast, manage at least the appearance of deep, openhearted attention.

If you are listening, if you are turning your big brown or blue eyes on somebody and twitching your ears at them, you are earning your silage. You are listening people into existence. You are saving lives. You are producing Grade A."

O'Reilley, *Radical Presence*, 29.

3 · EXPERIMENTS IN LISTENING

class can see at a glance how its members come out on a common question. Seeing how people disperse themselves on a line can be intriguing, and then being asked to listen actively to someone who's located herself at a different place from you can open your mind to a differing perspective. You might even change your mind.*

Although we probably all agree that listening is an exceptionally important skill for teachers and students, we think most of us and most of our students don't practice it very often. Most of the time, when someone else is talking, we either tune out or are so busy formulating our own responses to what she's saying that we don't listen to her. Our heads are too full of noise to be able to hear. By providing a structure for it, the 3 minutes each way strategy encourages us to listen carefully and actively to our conversational partners, and the experience of doing so may prompt us to transform how we listen and even how we think.

2. Wait Five Seconds before Responding

Have you ever found yourself aggravated in conversations, because your interlocutor continually interrupts you, never letting you complete your sentence, or responds so quickly you're certain he hasn't listened to what you're saying? Conversely, as mentioned above, when someone speaks to you, have you ever found yourself so busy formulating responses to what you're hearing that later you realize you haven't heard her? If so, the following story might interest you.

At a recent professors' reflection retreat,[20] people spent considerable time working in small groups. To help themselves get

---

* Compare Peter Elbow on the effects of playing the believing game.
    Something real and weighty goes on when we pay the believing game. The process often manages to change, genuinely if temporarily, the way we see and understand something. We literally "change our mind." That is, if we come to experience the full force of several competing views on a topic, to feel what it is like to believe each of those views, our final position is apt to change.
Elbow, *Embracing Contraries*, 270.

3 · EXPERIMENTS IN LISTENING

started, each group set explicit ground rules to help guide their conversations.[21] During their ground rules exercise, in one of those groups a participant noted that she tended to wait a few seconds after any comment in any discussion, and as a result, often felt left out of discussions, because what she might have wanted to say had been preempted by those who responded faster. She described that process and her subsequent attempt to keep track of the comment and insert it at a later, still appropriate point, which led her to become increasingly involved in an internal process of storing, sorting, and eventually eliminating comments that she felt unable to make or prevented from making. The overall effect was eventually to absent herself from those conversations, which sped along without her. Here's what she reported.

I'm not an introvert, and I'm not shy. I don't hesitate to voice my opinion. But when I work in a small group, I usually don't get to talk, because I HATE to interrupt—it feels disrespectful. My sense of the rhythm of conversation is different from others in my culture. If I wait what seems to me a respectful time after someone is done speaking, someone else has already started. That means if it's important to me to speak, I have to decide that I'm going to pounce on the end of someone else's speaking. To make that decision requires a conscious choice to disregard another's speaking space. That's a hard choice, and I have to steel myself for it. It usually takes some irritation to get me to that point, so when I do speak I sound (and sometimes am) angry.

After listening to her experience about listening, the group discussed how they might avoid this happening in their discussions, and they instituted the "five-second rule"; before anyone can respond to any comment, they must wait five seconds.

Everyone in the group, including the person whose experience prompted the rule, found using it transformed their conversation. Here's one particularly revealing response.

I was completely astonished by the way in which the five-second rule utterly changed my participation in our more

3 · EXPERIMENTS IN LISTENING

than six hours of group conversation that followed the adoption of this ground rule. I observed at least six separate things.

First, the five-second rule prevented me from interrupting. I sometimes literally had to clap my hand over my mouth to prevent myself from exclaiming in the middle of someone's comment.

On a second, related point, I found that I could no longer interject comments in order to try to reassure or change the affected flow of the conversation. For instance, in another setting, if friends of mine were making comments that were judgmental of themselves, I might be quick to interject, place a hand on their arm, or otherwise try to reassure them or even convince themselves to feel otherwise about the situation described.* The five-second rule prevented me from doing that.

---

* Compare this excerpt from a physician.

One of my patients told me that when she tried to tell her story, people often interrupted to tell her that they had once had something like that happen to them. Subtly her pain became a story about themselves. Eventually she stopped talking to most people. It was just too lonely. We connect through listening. When we interrupt what someone is saying to let them know that we understand, we move the focus of attention to ourselves. When we listen, they know we care. Many people with cancer talk about the relief of having someone just listen. I have learned to respond to someone crying by just listening. In the old days I used to reach for the tissues, until I realized that passing a person a tissue may just be another way to shut them down, to take them out of their experience of sadness and grief. Now I just listen. When they have cried all they need to cry, they find me there with them.

This simple thing has not been easy to learn. It certainly went against everything I had been taught since I was very young I thought people listen only because they were too timid to speak or did not know the answer. A loving silence has far more power to heal and to connect than the most well intentioned words.

Rachel Naomi Remen, M.D. *Kitchen Table Wisdom: Stories That Heal* (New York: Riverhead Books, 2002), 143–44.

Third, I noticed that the five-second rule prevented me in similar ways from pursuing other agendas of mine. For instance, in the second point related above, I realized that I had an ongoing agenda to show that I was empathetically listening, and to assure the person that I was on their side. The five-second rule prevented me from acting impulsively on that agenda, and actually acted to remind me that this was a point that need not be constantly reinforced. That is to say, I had a growing sense of confidence over time that my empathy and alliance with the other members of my small group was well understood and deeply felt, without my constant demonstration of it.

Fourth, as a result, as the person was speaking, I found myself settling deeper into the act of listening. I felt much less pressured to understand what the person was saying instantaneously (which, for instance, was required under the empathy agenda, because I needed to figure out quickly what the person was feeling in order to decide how I was going to respond or interject). Absent that agenda and a way to act on it, I found myself able to take in the thoughts and words expressed without formulating any immediate action plan.

Fifth, I found that during the actual five seconds of silence, my response changed. On at least a dozen occasions, I found myself at the beginning of the five second period with an immediate retort, quip or joke, which, as the silence grew, seemed suddenly inappropriate. It felt like it was stating the obvious, or on occasion, appearing to dismiss rather than engage the comment. In a complementary way, I often found myself at the beginning of the five seconds very concerned by the serious nature of a comment but at the end of the five second period able to see the issue with a bit more perspective and perhaps a sense of humor. That was especially true when I was the speaker and experienced in the five seconds of silence a sense of acceptance and an opportunity to see my own issues from a different perspective, before they were commented upon.

Sixth, when conversation began after the five seconds were up, the conversation tended to move in a slower, more reflective way than other conversations among the same group when the rules were not in effect. For instance, there was no banter, there were somewhat fewer jokes, and in my experience, there was a willingness to leave issues unresolved and open ended. If I were to summarize in a nutshell the most transformative aspect of this five-second rule for me, it was the freedom to listen deeply to another, and remove myself from the equation of describing or interpreting the event for a much longer period than I was usually able.

Of course the five-second rule was not always easy. I remember times when I clapped my hand over my mouth and swayed from side to side five times, or pressed my lips together and literally counted with my fingers to show that I was desperate to speak and only waiting the allotted time. At least one member of the group frequently stated his dislike of the rule, but also his conviction that he was learning something from it. In the end, I wondered if the surrounding of each comment by five seconds didn't give each comment a bit more gravity and provoked more thought about speaking and the direction in which any conversation would be taken.*

---

   * Although the group wasn't aware of it when it instituted the five-second rule, Peter Elbow has a related rule for methodological believing.

(T)here is a kind of "five-minute rule," which is a particularly easy way to try out methodological belief. A group can simply agree that whenever any participant feels that some idea or view is not getting a fair hearing, she can invoke the rule: for five minutes no criticism of the idea is permitted and everyone should try to believe it. Believing may seem impossible at first, but people can easily join in answering questions like these.

- What's interesting or helpful about the view? What are some of the intriguing features that others might not have noticed?
- What would you notice if you believed this view? If it were true?

86   3 · EXPERIMENTS IN LISTENING

3. Don't Offer Advice

Have you ever been in a conversation in which you're describing a problem you're experiencing, and your interlocutor jumps in to offer you advice on how to deal with it? Before you asked for his advice? On those occasions, did you always want advice, or did you simply want a sympathetic ear? Conversely, have you experienced yourself rushing to help your interlocutor solve her problem, assuming that's what she wants from you? What if that's not what she wants or needs?

Instead of intervening with advice, which can suggest to an interlocutor that you doubt their capabilities, what if you were to follow Mary Rose O'Reilley's suggestion at the beginning of this chapter and simply listen, deeply, open-heartedly. Perhaps that would be more helpful to our interlocutor, or when we are similarly situated, to ourselves. When we withhold our advice until we're asked and simply remain present to our friend, student, or colleague we're modeling for her our confidence that she has what she needs to solve her problem herself. In some circumstances, that can be a greater gift than our most thoughtful reflections on her problem.

4. Listen with Your Hands Occupied

"I listen better when I knit …"

Listening with hands occupied offers a listener a chance to experiment with the context in which listening takes place. For instance, some teachers who find students tongue tied in one-on-one conversations across the desk in their office, find students much more comfortable talking if they are driving to an event together or walking in the neighborhood of the school. Many knitters and craftspeople suggest that having their hands occupied,

---

   •   In what senses or under what conditions might this view be true?
Elbow, *Embracing Contraries*, 274–75.

while eliminating eye contact with the speaker, actually makes it easier to focus on what's being said. For them, what others might find distracting is just the reverse; it enhances their listening. In addition, the experience of a context in which other activities are being performed often creates a more comfortable environment for the speaker.

One way to think about this experiment in listening is suggested by the group exercise at the end of this essay. Take a critical incident of your listening and ask if it would have been different if it had happened while:

a. driving
b. cooking
c. doing a jigsaw puzzle
d. knitting
e. playing tennis or basketball
f. sharing a meal

5. *Practice Non-judgment*

Listening without expressing, or perhaps even feeling, judgment may offer fresh insight as well. Two experiments from legal practice literature may be helpful:

a. Active Listening—"Non-judgmental Acceptance"

One widely-used text on client interviewing and counseling suggests "active listening" techniques. When a client speaks, the actively listening lawyer is advised to reply by reflecting the "*essence* of the content of the client's remarks, as well as your perception, based on both on the statement and on the client's non-verbal cues, of the client's feelings. You distill the information and emotion from the client's statement, and then convey back what you have heard and understood–hence the term, 'active listening.'"[22]

Binder, Bergman and Price focus the lawyer on listening techniques that withhold judgment, that reflect back the client's view-

88   3 · EXPERIMENTS IN LISTENING

point. Teachers seeking active ways of encouraging students to speak freely can adopt a similar strategy.

b. Parallel Universes

As noted in Chapter 2, Jean and Sue Bryant have proposed a habit of "parallel universe" thinking for cross-cultural competence in lawyering.[23] The habit is simple: when confronting any new story, where few facts are known, brainstorm multiple explanations for the facts available. Thus, a teacher confronted with a student who has not delivered a paper as promised would imagine numerous parallel universes that might explain such lateness: a misunderstanding about the deadline, a computer problem, a family emergency, the paper completed but delivered to the wrong office. The goal of parallel universe thinking is not to brainstorm until the right answer is discovered, but rather to become aware of the vastness of the teacher's lack of data and knowledge, and to become open to the multiplicity of possible explanations involved. Parallel-universe thinking offers the listener an alternative to prejudgment, and invites listening without judgment—listening to understand, rather than to evaluate.

6. Try a Group Exercise

Many of the ideas above can be adapted for groups as well as individuals. Here is one example of a group exercise Mark and Jean used at various presentations of the early versions of this article.

Exploring Our Listening Together: A Group Exercise

Here's an exercise for a group of teachers. It takes anywhere from 30 minutes to an hour, and it's specifically designed to illustrate the experience of listening described in Section II B of this chapter, but it also implicates several other of the exercises.

Step 1: Recall a conversation with a student

Identify a conversation you recently have had with a student. You will be describing the conversation later to another partici-

3 · EXPERIMENTS IN LISTENING   89

pant. Be sure you can remember the conversation in some detail; try to remember at least part of it verbatim. Jot a few notes to recall this conversation and set it clearly in your mind.

Step 2: Create a Doubting/Believing Spectrum

The group should review the reading on the doubting and believing spectrum, which appears in Sections I A and II B. Using masking tape on the floor, the group can create a line-up depicting the spectrum. The masking tape line should be long enough to accommodate at the same time all participants in the group standing somewhere on the line. With masking tape, create a B at one side of the line and a D at the other side. Before people proceed to stand at the place on the line that signifies where they are on the spectrum, the group should make sure that everyone understands what constitutes pure doubting and pure believing, and understands what Elbow means by *methodological* doubting and believing.

Step 3. Find your place on the line

Recall your student conversation and think about the internal process (how you felt) and the external process (what you showed) of listening and conversing. Place yourself on the doubting and believing spectrum. The goal here is to find one point that makes sense to you as an accurate statement of where you would place yourself on the doubting and believing spectrum during this conversation. If you found that at certain moments you were at one part of the spectrum and other moments at another, pick a particular moment and use it to locate your place. If you find a contrast between your external and internal process, pick one and place yourself at one point. If you found yourself constantly moving between parts of the spectrum as you listened, and using some sort of average makes more sense, feel free to express that instead. If you must choose between your differing processes, choose your internal process over your external process.

Step 4. 3 minutes each way

Paired with another person for three minutes, and following the directions included above in Section II B (b), describe your conversation and explain why you placed yourself where you did on the spectrum. As a listener, do not respond in any way, even non-verbally. Then switch roles and listen to your partner for three minutes.

Step 5. Reflect on your experience

Reconvene the group. Return to your seats and your notes. Spend some time reflecting and jotting your responses to the following questions. Call your student conversation your *retrospective conversation* and your current conversation your *current experience of listening*. On your page, make a column for each:

Retrospective conversation   Current experience
with student   of listening

Answer each of the following questions for each experience of listening.

A. Prohibition on advice. Would your experience of listening have been different if you knew you would never be asked or allowed to offer advice about the situation?

B. With hands occupied. Would your experience of listening have been different if it had happened while you were:

a. driving?

b. taking notes?

c. doodling?

d. knitting?

e. making a salad?

f. fishing?

g. weeding a garden?

h. working on a jigsaw puzzle?

i. offer a similar example that fits into your life.

Theologian Henri Nouwen has described how he watched, in awe and wonder, as Philippe Petit walked a tightrope strung between a wall and the adjacent floor, only to realize, when Petit had finished, that the last length of rope had actually rested on the floor.[24] What he had just viewed with amazement was an act that he himself performed, without thinking or appreciation, dozens of times every day! In the same way, we view these experiments in listening as an opportunity to view with fresh eyes, and with a certain awe and wonder, the sophistication, complexity, and importance of this daily act of listening, which we perform dozens of times, every day in our lives.

We hope that several of these exercises have intrigued you and that performing them has led you to fresh insights about how you listen and possibly to think about changing some of your practices. As we've suggested, for us, the exercises suggest that a thoughtful listener has a set of listening modes, and in any setting, carefully chooses which mode they will use for listening. This listener uses a wide repertoire of skills and makes subtle, sophisticated choices about listening in each new context. At any moment, this listener is also conscious of distractions and obstacles and strategizes to eliminate impediments to optimal listening. Over time, with mindful attention to our processes, we can expand this repertoire and refine our listening.

What's most important to us is that you find strategies that work for you and help you explore your listening. There is something endlessly fascinating and challenging about this daily activity, and a reflective teacher may return to look at her listening practices fruitfully many times over a career. We encourage you to develop your own exercises, prompts, and analytical frameworks for a steady practice of exploring your listening through the years.

Notes

1. Mary Rose O'Reilley, *Radical Presence: Teaching as a Contemplative Practice* (Portsmouth, NH: Boynton/Cook, 1998), 19.

2. Pamela J. Cooper, *Communication for the Classroom Teacher*, 7th ed. (Boston: Allyn and Bacon, 2003), 65. The International Learning Association offers other statistics related to listening on its website, accessed January 20, 2011, http://d1025403.site.myhosting.com/files.listen.org/Facts.htm, and a list of interdisciplinary resources on listening: http://www.listen.org/Listening_Resources.

3. Ibid.

4. For an egregious example, see Stephen L. Carter's, *The Emperor of Ocean Park* (New York: Knopf, 2002), 111–14.

5. "In short, to use Polanyi's phrase, we know more tacitly than we do focally ..." Peter Elbow, "Teaching Two Kinds of Thinking by Teaching Writing," in *Embracing Contraries: Explorations in Learning and Teaching* (Oxford: Oxford University Press, 1986), 54. Elbow is a writing teacher and an extraordinary perceptive essayist on topics related to teaching and learning.

6. For ideas about journaling and free writing, consider the advice of Peter Elbow, *Embracing Contraries*, or Natalie Goldberg, a poet, novelist, writing teacher and author of *Wild Mind* (New York: Bantam, 1990).

7. Peter Elbow, "Methodological Doubting and Believing: Contraries in Inquiry," in *Embracing Contraries*, 253.

8. Ibid., 255.

9. Ibid., 258.

10. Ibid.

11. Ibid., 257.

12. Ibid., 261.

13. Ibid., 263.

14. Ibid., 283.

15. Ibid., 260.

16. We've adapted the high points/low points profile of best listeners prompt from Stephen Brookfield. Stephen D. Brookfield, *Becoming a Critically Reflective Teacher* (San Francisco: Jossey-Bass, 1995), 147–49, 77–78.

17. Elbow, *Embracing Contraries*, 258.

18. Ibid.

19. Louis Auchincloss, "Equitable Awards," in *Narcissa & Other Fables* (Boston: Houghton Mifflin Harcourt, 1983).

20. Tenth Annual Conference of the Institute for Law School Teaching, *Reflecting on Our Teaching*, held in Leavenworth, Washington July 2003.

21. For a useful model, see Stephen D. Brookfield, "Holding Critical Conversations About Teaching," in *Becoming a Critically Reflective Teacher* (San Francisco: Jossey-Bass, 1995), 143–45.

22. David A. Binder, Paul Bergman, and Susan C. Price, *Lawyers as Counselors: A Client-Centered Approach* (St. Paul: West Publishing, 1991), 53.

23. Susan Bryant, "The Five Habits: Building Cross-Cultural Competence in Lawyers," in *Clinical Law Review, vol. 8,* 33, and Jean Koh Peters, *Representing Children in Child Protective Proceedings: Ethical and Practical Dimensions,* 2nd ed. (Charlottesville: LexisNexis, 2001), 307.

24. Described by John Mogabgab, Nouwen's former teaching assistant, in Michael Ford, *Wounded Prophet: A Portrait of Henri J.M. Nouwen,* (New York: Doubleday, 1999), 25.

Chapter 4

Who Are Our Students, and How and What Do They Learn in Our Classrooms?

That's what teaching should be about but isn't: discerning the gift. Too often the central activity of our discipline is judging. The major thing we have learned to do in life is to assign grades.

—Mary Rose O'Reilley,
The Peaceable Classroom[1]

I. Who Were We as Students: Our Best/Worst Moments as Students

To judge and be judged—with grades, job searches, course evaluations, promotions, merit pay—that's what sometimes feels to be a university's central mission. Everyone judging everyone else.

In such a judging environment, what will we learn and who will we become? Which dimensions of ourselves will emerge, which will we submerge? What kinds of communities will we make? Will we and our students feel safe enough "to open ourselves to transformation,"[2] which Jane Tompkins argues is essential to learning? If not, then how can we help facilitate our students' and our own learning?

It might be useful to approach these questions by beginning with ourselves, the learners we know best. Who were we as students, and when did we learn most and least? Try this thought experiment.

96   4 · WHO ARE OUR STUDENTS?

Think back to one of your most satisfying experiences of learning, when you felt fully engaged, challenged, moving forward—whatever learning means for you. Jot down some notes. How old were you? Where were you during this experience? How much of your learning occurred in a classroom? Did anyone contribute to your learning? If so, how? What were you feeling during this experience? Etc.

Now do the same for one of your least satisfying, most frustrating, experiences.

As you look over what you've written, do any patterns emerge? How important was the environment? How important was your own emotional life at the time? To what extent were you in control of what you were learning? From what you observe, are there resonances for how you currently teach? Anything new you can bring to your own teaching? Anything you'd like to eliminate?

We know ourselves best, and it may be that what works for us works equally well for our students. However, they're differently situated from us: generationally, possibly emotionally, certainly in their training. Consequently, while our own experiences are a good place to begin, it's worth exploring who our students are: from their perspectives, and from others'. In the rest of the chapter, we will first listen to some students' voices, then explore how teachers sometimes participate in creating a culture of fear, and finally, propose some alternative strategies for facilitating our students' learning

II. Student Voices

Here are the voices of three students, expressing from differing perspectives their experiences of their education.* As you read, imagine yourself in the shoes of each of the protagonists.

A Family's Criminal Legacy[3]
Tanya Munro

---

* Selected from a group of essays written over several years in Mark's Legal Imagination class and published in the law journal, *Legal Studies Forum* 27 (2004): 371–438. While these are law student voices, we think they won't be completely unfamiliar to those of you in other disciplines.

4 · WHO ARE OUR STUDENTS?

I took a deep unsettling breath. My throat seized. I swallowed hard and tried to force stalled pockets of air into my lungs. Even to inhale required concentration. Greasing my fingers with saliva, I flipped through the pages of my first year criminal law book. My pulse quickened, and I dropped my chin closer to the book to disguise the spreading color on my face, as I quietly prayed against the inevitable. Believing that God overlooked me, I have never been a religious person. Yet, I hoped. My pleas for concealment were bargained without faith and proved futile. There it was—*R. v. Munro and Munro*, broadcast in bold black ink. I stared at my name, branded on page 404. I wanted to escape my skin. MUNRO. Munro, my new, inexorable, and apparently unavoidable identity. A dispassionate judicial narration of my bloodline was here casually exposed in print, my family legacy succinctly summarized in two pages. Carswell, the book publisher, had resurrected my history and distributed it en masse to the entire law school community. What I felt most was fear and shame, thoroughly humbled by my "white trash" origins. I did not consider infamy to be flattering attire for professional school. Would I have to submit to autograph signings after class?

I expected my fellow students to find me guilty by association, that my presence in law school had smudged that imaginary line between "good guys" and "bad guys." Smart, educated, good people go to law school. Law students are borne from doctors, philanthropists, accountants, teachers, and other lawyers. They are not descended from callous murders, rapists and common thieves. Law students read about criminals; they don't share DNA with them. I had become a double agent, caught in the big lie. My secrets unveiled, broadcasted, and scrutinized …

I found it to be an odd experience, to read about my family from a stranger's perspective. First, I noticed that judicial ink indifferently stamps names and describes events. Real people are vacant from the sober presentation of case law. In a legal rendition of life there are no fathers, uncles, or daughters, no broken homes, or beaten spirits. There are no stories of children kissing their father through walled prison plastic, or a child's silly preference for jails with vending machines that have their favorite candy. The pallid pages of the law book recite blunted facts and dramatize the logic of a legal argument. The reason the crime occurred—the real story the offender might tell–is nowhere to be found. In Stuart and Delisle's text— my Criminal Law Book—*R. v. Munro and Munro* is lined-up with the other cases in Chapter 3, "The Fault Requirement," nonchalantly placed under the heading, "Murder of a Police Officer." The placement may be logical, but it seemed glaringly out of place to me.

I must say I know very little about my branch of the Munro family. My sister is the only Munro I have any kind of relationship with. Newspaper clippings, old court documents, and snippets of information pinched from private conversations have filled the gaps in my memory. My father was the oldest son of Lawrence and Francis Munro's eleven children. I derived this information from his death certificate, which I obtained from the registrar under false pretenses. It is a curious world that prevents a daughter from knowing where her father is buried. Of the eleven children in my father's family only three managed to avoid criminal sanctions. It was a family of habitual offenders leading self-destructive lives. The court did not ask why or how this happened. There will be some who attribute it to genetic predisposition, an hereditary propensity for violence. This answer frightens me, makes me wary of myself. But I'm not convinced it's the right answer. There was also chronic alcoholism and substance abuse, but how this got to be the norm in the family I cannot say. The better explanation is that it was a family which revolved around emotional and physical abuse. In the Munro household abuse often substituted for love. As a child my father had been beaten to the point of unconsciousness.

It left him filled with hate and anger. Returning as an adult to that childhood home, he saturated its planks with gasoline and burnt it to the ground. A symbolic act, accomplishing nothing.

I often wonder what kind of person my father might have been if someone had tried to save him, or if anyone knew enough to try to save the children by removing them from harm. But no one did anything, and now eight siblings are criminal justice system darlings. The story of these children and the pain they must all bear is totally missing from the court records. It's ironic that the public and the government complain about the cost of maintaining the prison system, when their disregard helps create the people who inhabit it.

I remember walking the shiny halls of a correctional facility as a child, trying to stomp on the gleam reflected on the floor from the fluorescent lights overhead. I was oblivious to the fact that my father was in jail because he was a bad man. It was normal for me to speak to him through the awkward black phone hanging alongside the thick plastic wall separating us. Such things should never be normal, but then these things should never happen.

I now look upon *R. v. Munro and Munro* as a personal documentary, as a synopsis of a defunct lineage and my strained identity. Given that this case is of obvious personal significance, I have not tried to discuss its legal issues as would a law student. Instead of focusing on what is written in the judgment, I have been compelled by what it does not say. It may appear that I wish to shift the responsibility for my family's crimes to someone else. Perhaps I want to vindicate my father, or better, change the past. And I will always wonder whether a family of Munro children provided with a safe and loving home might not have averted the murder of police officer Sweet and many other crimes. I would have a father, and perhaps it this unsatisfied desire that motivates my writing.

Gantarro Tower[4]
Stephanie Mah

My travels upon departure from Lilliput had hitherto been a pleasant diversion, when they suddenly took a turn for which I was quite unprepared. At some equal distance between Lilliput and Blefescu, I stumbled upon a most amazing and wondrous spectacle. Before me stood a glistening tower, so polished and smooth I could not be sure it was not an earthbound sun. It was the tallest building I had encountered during my travels, so tall I feared it might interrupt the slow journey of some unfortunate clouds.

Amassed outside the tower at its base were sundry birds. I saw the more common: chickens, crows, pigeons, sparrows, and geese, and the exotic: parrots, toucans, and flamingos. There were others I could not recognize. All of them were in an excited state, and I was curious to know the reason. I approached the gathering of fowl and began to inquire, but none of them would deign to speak with me; indeed, none of them were speaking with each other. Perhaps they did not understand my questions, but it was not a look of puzzlement that greeted my inquiries, rather disdain. I did not have a chance to press further, as all the birds alerted me to something happening at the tower.

There was [a] most glorious peacock, with feathers so royal blue that it was hard to see against the deepening black hues of the evening sky. The green of the peacock's feathers reminded me of jade. Surrounded in the great beauty of his feathers, he began to address the audience.

"Those of you who wish to be admitted are already aware of the conditions you must meet; let us begin."

To my astonishment and amusement, at this pronouncement the assembled birds began to leap as high as they could. It was a rather absurd sight. The chickens fared poorly at the leaping, while the long-limbed flamingos had an easy go of it. The dodos seemed totally inept at the task. I was puzzled why none of the birds took flight, but that did not deter me from taking part in the lunacy—I too leapt and was better at it than the birds. The sun was drawing its path across the sky and the evening was coming upon us when, finally, the peacock spoke again.

"We have made our selection." With that said, he began gesturing towards the successful leapers, me among them. The great doors at the base of the tower opened before us, and the chosen began to enter. Those who were not selected seemed to be in great distress. My curiosity outweighing my sympathy, I entered the great tower.

As the exterior of the great tower had been so magnificent, I expected the interior to be equally dazzling, but I was greatly disappointed. The interior was quite soiled, and the walls were cracked and smeared with filth; the floor was massively scuffed, grooved, and worn; the ceilings were buckling; there was a general sense of stagnancy. Yet none of the fowl seemed to notice this condition.

We were ushered to a great hall by several other peacocks, none of whom equaled the colored, plumed splendor of the one who had spoken. One of the peacocks addressed us. "Welcome to Gantarro Tower. I am Master Weryal. I am certain you realize the great honor it is to be a resident of this Tower, and I assure you that once you have completed your three day stay, you shall have acquired many great skills."

Most of that first day in Gantarro was devoted to teaching the birds how to bark. From throughout the tower one could hear clucking, cawing, chirps, coos, whistles, and barking. Those who could not bark were held in great contempt. I had the opportunity to ask one of the masters what the meaning of the barking was, but he could offer no sufficient answer, save for this: "meaning matters not, what matters is who can bark the loudest and with the greatest conviction."

The second day in Gantarro the birds progressed from their efforts to learn to bark to participation in some kind of game. I cannot state with certainty that it was a game, I only infer it, as it seemed to result in those who were victorious and those who met with misfortune. The game seemed to involve elements of pageantry, and there was some enjoyment in watching the display of the well-groomed, excited fowl. But there were outbreaks of jealousy and vanity which led to altercations between the birds.

The third day in Gantarro was spent in absolute idleness. Most of the fowl lazed about, stopped barking, and drank of a liquid that seemed to induce a higher level of idiocy than already existed.

Ascension Day was a cause of great excitement, and what took place was perhaps the most bizarre scene I have ever witnessed. One by one, each of the birds allowed himself to be hoisted up by the legs, so that he was suspended upside down over the ground. So positioned, the masters would approach him and begin to tear the feathers from the body, until the bird was left savagely pink and quaking, perhaps from the unfamiliar coolness or from what I must imagine would be the great pain resulting from the plucking. Yet despite the ordeal, the bird was silent. Next, the masters slathered on a salve on the body of the bird, which I took to be some sort of adhesive, for after its application, the masters began to attach to each of the birds, peacock feathers. Each bird emerged from this plucking and gluing looking all the worse for having been stripped of its natural plumage, only to have it replaced with peacock feathers, arranged in the most haphazard fashion. It was only as Ascension Day drew to a close that I took a closer look at the masters themselves, and realized that some of them, too, seemed to be imposters.

I had not discovered this earlier, because the peacock feathers on the masters had been applied with much greater care, in greater quantity, and with some idea of replicating the look of a real peacock.

Finally, the great doors of Gantarro Tower were thrown open and the birds, in a state of bewilderment, were told to exit. I, too, took my leave, and puzzled over the various scenes of deception I had witnessed, and wondered at the havoc these birds might wreak upon the world.

Sui Generis[5]
Lisa Fong

"... and it is *sui generis.*" Accordingly I scribbled down '... and it is *sui generis.*' But I didn't know what *sui generis* meant. I looked around the class to see if anyone else looked bewildered. It appeared not, since everyone else was busy taking down the professor's next words, something I should have been doing. For a moment I thought about putting my hand up and asking what *sui generis* meant, but I didn't want to interrupt the lecture or disturb the other students who apparently did not share the problem I was having. I assumed it must just be a complex sounding Latin phrase for a simple legal concept. So I decided that I could wait and ask the professor after class.

"... and for next week read pages ..." The professor ended the class with our next reading assignment. I collected my books and made my way down to the front of the class to ask what *sui generis* means. There were two other students lined up to talk to the professor and one talking to him. I lined up behind them. He looked at the three of us after finishing with the first student and said that we should sign up to see him during office hours since he didn't have time to talk to us right now. He said this while he was putting on his jacket, collecting his lecture notes, and heading out the door.

I figured that my question could be so quickly and easily answered that the professor wouldn't mind me showing up at his office for a quick question. When I arrived at his office and knocked on the door, there was no answer. It appeared that he had not bothered returning to his office before leaving the building. The notice on the door said that he would be out of town giving a lecture until the following week. While I could easily look up the meaning of *sui generis* at the library, our exams were only two weeks away, and I was sure that after studying the whole week-end I would have other questions.

With my professor absent, I headed off to the library to find out the meaning of *sui generis* and met my friend Kirsten along the way. I asked her if she knew what *sui generis* meant. She shrugged and said I should ask my professor or look it up at the library. I didn't feel like explaining that I had already tried to ask my professor and was on my way to the library to look up the term. She asked if I had read the article in the Queen's Journal criticizing the law school curriculum. I hadn't. So she explained that the author of the article had complained that law students were not learning "black letter law" and there were too many tempting "soft law" courses being offered. The author claimed that the legal profession was in danger of being overrun with lawyers who didn't have a firm grasp of basic legal principles. Listening to Kirsten talk about this article, I wondered if I was going to be one of those inadequate lawyers. Not only did I not know what *sui generis* meant (which apparently my classmates did), but I was taking one of those soft law courses. Perhaps if I had taken Insolvency instead of Professor Weisberg's Legal Imagination seminar, I would know what *sui generis* meant.

I excused myself from Kirsten and made a dash to the library. It was closed. I looked down at my watch and saw that it was just past five o'clock. I would have to wait 'till ten o'clock the next morning to find out what *sui generis* means.

Later that night I had a disturbing dream. In the dream the word had gotten out at school that I didn't know what *sui generis* meant. This was bad for the school. The author's criticism of the law school curriculum and its "soft law" courses was bolstered by the fact that one of the school's future representatives did not know an important principle of *real* law. This caused such great concern that the Dean decided to send out a posse to save me.

The Dean calls to tell me to expect his team of *sui generis* experts. He then suggests that if after my work with them, I still don't know what *sui generis* means, then I should consider taking a term off and seeking a better grounding in analytic theory.

His suggestion scared me. I didn't want to take time off from law school to seek training in formal logic, scientific rationality, the art of war, crossword puzzle theory, or whatever it was he meant by "analytic theory." So I dressed in my Sunday best, had a cup of carrot juice to invigorate my brain, and waited for my visitors.

The first sign of them was a huge cloud of black smoke on the horizon. As the smoke moved closer, I saw that it spewed forth from a rickety old yellow school bus with a giant Queens' insignia on the front and side. I could see the faces of my visitors pressed against the windows of the bus. They looked all pasty and in need of fresh air and lots of carrot juice. The bus pulled up in front of my house, came to a noisy stop, issued a final great puff of black smoke, and proceeded to let off her passengers.

The first person out was Norm, a fellow classmate in my *sui generis* class. He rushed through my front door, grabbed my arm, and led me to the kitchen table. I offered him a glass of carrot juice, but he said he didn't have time to drink anything. After his work with me, he had to get back to studying for final exams. He explained that our professor was away giving a lecture on a cutting-edge issue of law and had dispatched him to help me with my problem. He flipped open his notebook, muttered "ahh … *sui generis*," flipped some pages, and then closed his notebook. Then, reaching out to hold my hands, he looked into my eyes and told me that *sui generis* was a highly complex and philosophical concept that I didn't need to know to pass the course. He said, "if it wasn't exam period right now I could take the time to explain it to you. But you know how it is. We need to take care of our own interests. Besides, it's only a small part of the course and might not even be on the examination, and even if it is, I'm sure your other courses will balance out your average if you don't do well in this course." He wished me luck on the exam and left.

I had another glass of carrot juice. It occurred to me that I was expecting too much of my professor and his dispatched surrogate, Norm, to take the time to teach me something so complex. After all, the time that a professor has for someone like me is limited; he has his own goals in life to pursue. My professor was an author and a lecturer, and I had to expect that he would need time for his research, writing, and lecturing. And it wasn't as if he neglected his students. He showed up for all his lectures (except when he was away lecturing), was well organized for those lectures (he always read from his prepared notes), and answered all questions asked in class (there weren't many questions; he had a smart class). Norm was much like our professor. In fact, it was clear that he too strove to be a professor. That was why he took on the added burden of tutoring first year law students. It must have been hard on Norm to not be able to take the time to teach me *sui generis*. But Norm, like the rest of us, has to prioritize, and exams come first, especially if he is to become a professor.

I looked out the kitchen window, hoping that the daisies in the window box would cheer me up. It was then that I saw that the Dean had sent the entire Faculty Council, who when they trooped into my kitchen, just about filled the entire space.

The Chairwoman sat in the seat that Norm had vacated. She declared that there was something wrong with the school system if I hadn't learned *sui generis* in my first year and was still unable to learn it now. She said she suspected that it had to do with my not being able to ask in class what *sui generis* meant. Perhaps the classes were so large that I felt alienated? Or could it be that the classroom was too adversarial? Or perhaps the professor did not welcome questions? She seemed to genuinely want to know what it was that impeded my learning.

I was both relieved and startled by her concerns. I was relieved, because someone seemed to care enough to try to find out if there was a reason why I wasn't learning the way I should. And I was startled, because I didn't have ready answers for all these big questions. The minutes passed as I tried to organize my thoughts about what it was that I found disadvantageous to my learning in the classroom situation. I could see that the members of the Board were waiting for my answers.

Then suddenly the ripple of a paper bag broke the silence. Out of the paper bag came an 8×10 exam booklet. The Chairwoman placed it on the table in front of me and said that I obviously needed to take an exam on these questions. When I had thought the questions through, I was to write down my answers in the booklet and hand it in to the council. They then left.

After the Faculty Council left, there was a knock at the back door. I got up and answered it. It was a Federal Express courier with a same-day delivery letter. I signed for the letter, closed the door, and opened the envelope. It was a request from the author of the article criticizing the legal curriculum at Queens to tell my story to the public. He wanted me to disclose my academic background, enumerate the soft law courses I was taking, and admit to the world that I did not learn what *sui generis* was in my time at law school. He said it was my moral responsibility to the public to let them know how members of the legal profession were being trained. He hoped that if I spoke up, there would still be enough time for the system to change to save people like me.

After the dream I needed more carrot juice. The author was wrong. My not learning the concept of *sui generis* was not because I had taken Legal Imagination instead of Insolvency. It was because I could not ask my professor in class what the concept meant. It was because I could not ask my professor out of class what the concept meant. It was because anyone I asked either didn't know or didn't have the time to explain it to me. It was because the library was closed for the night.

I poured myself another glass of carrot juice as I wondered why communication in the classroom was so difficult for me. The classes were, no doubt, too large for comfortable discussion. Some students simply didn't want to disturb the rest of the class or sought out the professor for a private discussion. Others thought it inappropriate to interrupt a lecture. Still others didn't want to show their lack of knowledge to classmates. And some didn't want to participate in a debating session, where one student could appear victorious (and smarter than others), while the class sat as spectators to the sport, cheering on the combatants. Sometimes the competition was skewed by the fact that the professor was one of the debaters. He always won.

Whatever the communication problems in [the] classroom, I had no good excuse not to go to the library to research the meaning of *sui generis*. But this solution, good enough for a *sui generis* problem, might not be so effective in correcting a mistake about a legal concept. Even when you get something dead wrong on an examination, there is no effort to make sure you ever understand the problem. Most exams are not returned, and when they are, there are few, if any, comments. With this system of examination there is no way to correct and discuss your errors and misconceptions; no way to learn from your mistakes.

I remember the end of the dream now. A loud roar comes from the front yard, and black smoke starts drift-

4 · WHO ARE OUR STUDENTS?   109

ing into the kitchen from the window. It's the old Queen's
school bus revving up to leave. I run outside, hoping to
catch one of the Faculty Council members, since I still
don't know what *sui generis* means. But I'm too late. The
smoke-belching contraption rolls away, the faces of its oc-
cupants pressed against the window.

———————

Imagine each of these students in one of your classes. As their
teacher, you won't know what they're experiencing, but you will
know that as they arrive, several of them might be bringing similar feelings. Will that matter to you? If so, can you imagine what
you and your class might do to prevent these feelings or experiences from interfering with their learning and with their classmates' learning? Jot down any ideas you have. We'll return to this
topic in Section IV below.

III. A Culture of Fear and Its Consequences

What does it mean for learning to live in a culture in which
we're always concerned with being judged and always judging others. Here are three examples expressing how it might feel to students, and two more expressing how it might feel to us.

A. Three Classrooms, Three Nightmare Scenarios

Expecting Adam[6]
Martha N. Beck

.... [My son, who had Down's Syndrome] had a way
of looking at the heart of things, from stopping to smell
not only the roses but the bushes as well. It is a quality of
attention to ordinary life that is so loving and intimate it
is almost worship. At Harvard,* of course, I had learned
to pay attention to very different things. The importance

———————

* Beck was a graduate student at Harvard.

of prestige is so overwhelming in that culture that people hardly look at each other, let alone their environment. The attention goes to appearances: appearing successful, appearing smart, appearing utterly and absolutely unlike a retarded child.

I began to notice this when I was pregnant with Adam, months before I had any solid evidence that there was anything 'different' about him. Maybe his way of seeing, the depth of his appreciation for life, seeped from him into my bloodstream, or maybe it was the immediate proximity of his soul that affected mine. Whatever the reason, things began to look different.

It was mid-November and the few remaining leaves rattled on the trees. I welcomed the winter chill, since ice air helped keep my mind off the nausea. I breathed it carefully one day as I waddled over to William James Hall (known to the intelligentsia as Billy Jim) to attend a class. I arrived a few minutes early and decided to use the extra time to visit a friend in the Psychology Department, one floor above the Sociology Department, where my class was held. My friend was in her lab, conducting an experiment that consisted of implanting wires into the brains of live rats, then making the rats swim around in a tub of reconstituted dry milk. She told me why she was doing this, but I have no memory of what she said. Maybe she was making soup. Whatever the reason, she had put the rats and the milk in a children's wading pool, the kind you fill up with a hose so that toddlers can splash around on a hot summer day. The tub was decorated with pictures of Smurfs. Smurfs, for those of you who are not culturally aware, are little blue people whose antics you may have observed on Saturday morning cartoons during the 1980s. I personally feel that the Smurfs were cloying, saccharine little monsters, but [my daughter] Katie adored them.

After chatting with my rat-molesting friend for a moment, I excused myself and headed downstairs for the seminar. There were seven or eight other graduate students in attendance, along with a couple of extra professors who had come to hear the latest twist on established theories. I felt the way I always did when I walked into a classroom at Harvard, that I had just entered a den of lions—not starving lions, perhaps, but lions who were feeling a little peckish. The people in the room were fearsomely brilliant, and I was always terrified that I would say just one completely idiotic thing, make one breathtakingly asinine comment that would expose me as a boorish, politically incorrect half-wit.

"Ah, Martha," said the course instructor, "we've been waiting for you."

I blushed. I had stopped at the rest room to blow a few chunks, and had been hoping that the class would start a bit late. I did not want to be the focus of attention.

"I'm sorry," I said. "I was upstairs in the Psych lab, watching rats swim around in a Smurf pool."

"I see," said the instructor, "Yes, I believe I've read about that."

A professor, one of the visiting dignitaries, chimed in. "How is Smurf's work going?" he inquired. "I understand he's had some remarkable findings."

"Yes," said a graduate student. "I read his last article."

There was a general murmur of agreement. It seems that everyone in the room was familiar with Dr. Smurf, and his groundbreaking work with swimming rats.

It took me a few discombobulated seconds to figure out that everyone at the seminar assumed a Smurf pool was named for some famous psychological theorist. I guess they thought it was like a Skinner box, the reinforcement chamber used by B. F. Skinner to develop the branch of psychological theory known as behaviorism. Comprehension blossomed in my brain like a lovely flower.

I think," I said solemnly, "that Smurf is going to change the whole direction of linguistic epistemology."

They all agreed, nodding, saying things like 'Oh, yes,' and "I wouldn't doubt it."

I beamed at them, struggling desperately not to laugh. It wasn't so much that I wanted to mock these people. I was giddy with exhilaration, because after seven years at Harvard, I was just beginning to realize that I wasn't the only one faking it. I had bluffed my way through many a cocktail party, pretending to know all about whichever scholar or theory was the current topic of conversation. I had always wondered how I survived among the staggeringly intelligent people lurking all around me. Now I was beginning to understand.

"He's a good man, Smurf is," said the instructor solemnly.

And thus I learned that at Harvard, while knowing a great deal is the norm and knowing everything is the goal, appearing to know everything is considered an acceptable substitute.

The Emperor of Ocean Park[7]
A Novel by Stephen L. Carter

And so it is that on this, my first day back in the classroom, I find myself persecuting an unfortunate young man whose sin is to inform us all that the cases I expect my students to master are irrelevant, because the rich guys always win. Now, it is true that some poor fool announces this conclusion every fall, and it is also true that more than a few professors have earned tenure at some very fine law schools by pressing refined, jargon-chunky versions of precisely this thin theory; but I am in no mood for blather. I glare at the cocky student and see, for a horrible moment, the future, or maybe just the enemy: young, white, confident, foolish, skinny, sullen, multiply pierced, bejeweled, dressed in grunge, cornsilk hair in ponytail, utterly the cynical conformist, although he thinks he is an iconoclast. A few generations ago, he would have been the fellow wearing his letterman's sweater inside out, to prove to everybody how little it meant to him. When I was in college, he would have been first to the barricades, and he would have made sure everybody saw him there. As he is sure everybody is looking at him now. His elbow is on his chair, his other fist in tucked under his chin, and I read in his posture insolence, challenge, perhaps even the unsubtle racism of the supposedly liberal white student who cannot quite bring himself to believe that his black professor could know more than he. About anything. A light frosty red dances around his face like a halo, and I catch myself thinking, I could break him. I remind myself to be gentle.

"Very interesting, Mr. Knowland," I smile, taking a few steps down the aisle toward the row in which he sits. I fold my arms. "Now, how does your very interesting thesis relate to the case at hand?"

Still leaning back, he shrugs, barely meeting my gaze. He tells me that my question is beside the point. It is not the legal rules that matter, he explains to the ceiling, but the fact that workers cannot expect justice from the capitalist courts. It is the structure of the society not the content of the rules, that leads to oppression. He may even be half right, but none of it is remotely relevant, and his terminology seems as outdated as a powdered wig. I pull an old pedagogical trick, inching closer to crowd his field of vision, forcing him to remember which of us is in a position of authority I ask him whether he recalls that the case at hand involves not an employee suing an employer but one motorist suing another. Mr. Knowland, twisted around in his chair, answers calmly that such details are distractions, a waste of our time. He remains unwilling to look at me. His posture screams disrespect, and everybody knows it. The classroom falls silent even the usual sounds of pages turning and fingers clacking on laptop keyboards and chairs scraping disappear. The red deepens. I recall that I had to upbraid him three weeks ago for fooling around with his Palm Pilot during class. I was circumspect then, taking care to call him over after the hour ended. Still, he was angry, for he is of the generation that assumes that there are no rules but those each individual wills. Now, through the crimson haze, my student begins to resemble Agent McDermott as he sat, lying through his teeth, in the living room at Shepard Street ... and, very suddenly, it is too late to stop. Smiling as insolently as Mr. Knowland, I ask him whether he has undertaken a study of the tort cases, sorting them by the relative wealth of the parties, to learn the truth or falsity of his theory. Glaring, he admits that he has not. I ask him whether he is aware of any such study performed by anybody else. He shrugs. "I will take that as a no," I say, boring into him now. Standing right in front of his table, I tell him that there is, in fact, a substantial literature on the effect of wealth on the outcome of cases. I ask him if he has read any of it. The antiquated fluorescent lights buzz and hiss uncertainly as we wait for Mr. Knowland's reply. He looks around the classroom at the pitying faces of his classmates, he looks up at the portraits of prominent white male graduates that line the walls, and at last he looks back at me.

"No," he says, his voice much smaller. I nod as through to say I knew it all along. Then I cross the line. As every mildly competent law professor knows, this is the point at which I should segue smoothly back into the discussion of the case, perhaps teasing Mr. Knowland a little by asking another student to act as his co-counsel, in order to help him out of the jam into which he has so foolishly talked himself. Instead, I give him my back and move two paces away from his seat, then whirl and point and ask him whether he often offers opinions that have no basis in fact. His eyes widen, in frustration and childlike hurt. He says nothing, opens his mouth, then shuts it again, because he is trapped: no answer that he can give will help him. He looks away again as his classmates try to decide whether they should laugh. (Some do, some do not.) My head pounds redly and I ask: "Is that what they taught you at—Princeton, wasn't it?" This time, the students are too shocked to laugh. They do not really like the arrogant Mr. Avery Knowland, but now they like the arrogant Professor Talcott Garland even less. In the abrupt, nervous silence of the high-ceilinged classroom, it strikes me, far too late, that I, a tenured professor at one of the best law schools in the land, am in the process of humiliating a twenty-two-year-old who was, all of five years ago, in high school—the campus equivalent of a sixth-grade bully beating up a kindergartner. It does not matter if Avery Knowland is arrogant or ignorant or even is he is racist. My job is to teach him, not to embarrass him. I am not doing my job.

My rampant demons have chased me even into my classroom.

I soften once more. And try to clean up the mess. Of course, I continue, tweedily pacing the front of the room, lawyers are occasionally called upon to argue what they cannot prove. But—and here I spin and stiletto my finger again toward Mr. Knowland—but, when they offer these unsupported and unsupportable arguments, they must do so with verve. And they must have the confidence, when asked about the factual basis of their claims, to do the courtroom polka, which I demonstrate as I repeat the simple instructions: sidestep, sidestep, sidestep, stay on your toes, and never, ever face the music.

Relieved, jittery laughter from the students.

Except a glaring Avery Knowland.

I am able to finish the class, even to summon a bit of dignity, but I flee to my office the instant noon arrives, furious at myself for allowing my demons to drive me to embarrass a student in class. The incident will reinforce my reputation around the law school—not a nice person, the students tell each other, and Dana Worth, the faculty's foremost connoisseur of student gossip, cheerfully repeats it to me—and maybe the reputation is the reality.

4 · WHO ARE OUR STUDENTS?

The Vocation of a Teacher[8]
Wayne Booth

At the same time, and with only seeming paradox, teaching is a life that offers daily temptations to egotistical triumph. This obstacle to real teaching is more easily satirized than discussed sympathetically (as I tried to do in "The Good Teacher as Threat," Occasion 18 below). A class of eighteen-year-olds, each of whom knows that "success in life" depends in part on how this absolute dictator assigns final grades, can be the most misleading of all captive audiences except cowed citizens in a police state. How can they not laugh at my jokes—so long as I make them obvious enough? How can they not use flattery, subtle or blatant?

Here is an attempt to show how that works, in a freshman class-hour excerpted from my someday-perhaps-to-be-completed novel, Cass Andor. Jeremiah Gemissant, a minor character, is in effect showing the world how much smarter he is than poor Cass, a freshman who has made the mistake of baring his soul in his first assigned essay:

Assistant Professor Gemissant was playing one of his favorite games, Stamping out Naïveté, and most of the kids in the class were loving it, and him. It was one of the moments when he felt best about his teaching, this moment late in the second week or early in the third, when he read aloud from one of the more amusing essays and commented as he read. Bursts of laughter were by now greeting every sentence, whether from the essay itself or from his witty commentary. But it had taken a few moments of careful guidance to bring them to this point of bloodthirstiness.

Here is what they had heard so far:

"Some people feel that you can make conclusions about life itself or about the whole modern world of today by looking at written evidence like what you find in newspapers."

4 · WHO ARE OUR STUDENTS?

"Whenever I read a phrase like 'some people think' I wonder, which people? Does the author have anyone in mind, really? If so, why doesn't he or she … incidentally, I should just mention that I make it a point always to preserve the anonymity of the student when I read from a paper, unless the student himself, or herself, chooses to break the secret." Cass was already blushing so deeply that anyone looking at her knew the paper was hers.

"But as I was saying, who are 'some people'? Nobody, that's who." Only a smile or two, so far; they're not getting it. "'Some people feel'… the author surely means think, since there are no feelings mentioned." Still only faint smiles. "… 'that you can make conclusions'—I wonder if the author has asked himself or herself whether to 'make a conclusion' is a better thing to do than simply to conclude?"

Gemissant has mastered, self-consciously, that special rising intonation used by the younger generation to turn an indicative sentence into a bland interrogative, with a rising diphthong. "And I conclude that the author has not thought about it at all, but simply felt that to 'make a conclusion' is somehow fancier and thus more appropriate to college-level discourse than to conclude.

"Conclusions about life itself?" Anybody know any life that is not life itself?" Titters. "But life itself does sound somehow more imposing, so it was slapped down, again presumably because it felt good." More titters; now we're coming; they're getting the pitch.

"'About the whole modern world of today'? Now we're beginning to discover the pattern of a kind of mind here, folks. 'Life itself' and 'the whole world.' Like wow!" Real laughter at last.

So now he had them; every sentence a boffo. An act like that can go on for a long time, even if you're not the victim. So I spare you, as Cass was not spared, his comment on her second sentence: "But anybody who thinks about it all will see that newspapers report mainly the bad things about life of the world." But here he is again, on the third:

"'The old saying goes, if dog bites man, no news; if man bites dog, that's news.' I must say, class, that I've been reading student papers now for five years, and I had begun to hope that I'd live my professional life to the end without having to read that tired saying for the one-hundred-and-fiftieth time. But here it is, and the self-protection of 'the old saying' doesn't really help it much."

And the fourth:

"'Well, I would like to suggest ...' Well, if you'd sort of like to suggest, why don't you go ahead and suggest instead of backing into the sentence this way, like a shy high school girl going to her first prom." Real guffaws now; got em! But many of those who were laughing hardest were by now—and Jeremiah Gemissant did not know this, indeed never discovered this to his retiring day—already inwardly drying up, thinking: If he objects to all that, nothing, nothing I can ever say can get past him, let alone please him. I'm doomed, doomed, we're all doomed, but meanwhile let's make sure that this rival is dead; grading here will be of degrees of badness, and let us hope this is the worst.

"'... that the saying should read, if man strokes dog and dog returns stroke with deep and lasting affection, no news: if dog bites man, news—if the man is an important citizen; if dogs bites man and has rabies, then that's news!' Note how the epigrammatic quality of the original saying, banal as it is, has now been turned into preachy sententiousness." Alas, there was no one there to note that Gemissant was allowing himself certain stylistic latitudes denied to all the rest.

"But let us hurry on, 'I would suggest ...' Oh, no, not again, shy creature ..."

And so on Assistant Professor Jeremiah Gemissant went, line by line, phrase by phrase, through the most miserable hour of Cass's hitherto almost carefree life.

4 · WHO ARE OUR STUDENTS?   119

The self-flattery can spill over from class to paper-grading time. How smart can Jeremiah appear to himself, sitting alone with red pencil flashing?

Mechanics: B
Style: C
Argument: F

Dorcas Andor
Freshman Humanities
October 5, 1967
Mr. Gemissant

A good clean paper, Cass— but one that says nothing. I'm afraid we must talk about it.

What I believe most strongly:

meaning?

all?
Hitler?

What I believe most strongly is that the universe is love, and that all human beings deserve love and can learn from love. God created the world so that people could learn how to love and how to learn, and he gave every person the essential equipment for progress in love. The misery in the world is caused because people have failed to give other people the love that they need. If everybody would just work harder in loving, the main troubles of the world would be solved—e.g., war, crime, political conniving-all these are obviously the direct result of lack of love.

even idiots?

redundant

Why don't they of God created them?

evidence?

evidence?

I believe, secondly, that the world is progressing. Though there have been many ups and downs throughout recorded history, on the whole, more and more people are learning the importance of love, and practicing love in the world. Though I have already read in this course some authors who think the world is getting worse rather than better, to me what they say seems just silly. Everybody I know of is constantly improving, except for those who have not been given the love they need. Sometimes when I think of the whole universe, getting better and better as more and more people learn how to love, I could almost burst with the feeling of being part of all that. And I sometimes cannot help wondering, when it feels so wonderful to me, why so many people take so long in discovering the joys of love and progress. This is one of those things I would like to find out what is holding things back
Third and last, I believe in education. There is so much to learn that everyone can have a whole life time of learning if he wants it. And if there is a life after death (I don't list that as something I believe strongly, but it seems to me the

name calling not evidence!

proof?

look up "sentimentality"

weak

wordy

pn

new topic?

> most plausible hypothesis of all hypotheses
> I can think of) then we could go on
> learning forever, and that would to me be
> a great thing. I can't believe that God
> would plan (this) desire for eternal learning
> and growing in me and then frustrate it by
> making my death from this life final.
> Surely there is a (divine plan) that
> includes all my beliefs and many more that
> I will learn about in my next life.

Margin annotations (handwritten):
evidence? · *not clear why* · *antecedent?* · *you grow shrill here.* · *Is it because you suspect that you are talking nonsense?* · *new topic?*

As you can see, there's not much being learned in these classrooms, unless it's learning not to risk being present. For fear of being mistaken, students can act in ways that later will embarrass them. And if they're willing to be controlled by their fear in university environments, where the downside risk is relatively low, how will they respond when the risks increase?

In the first scenario, the pressures are implicit. Go where the teacher goes. In the latter two, it's explicit. Follow me, or else.

How much of what we do in our classrooms contributes, implicitly or explicitly, to a fear-driven environment? As the Carter and Booth fictional excerpts demonstrate, students aren't the only ones who bring their history and their emotions with them into our classes; so do we. Like psychiatrists and many other professionals, teachers can't escape issues of counter-transference.[9] Most of us have experienced moments when we project onto a student, or an entire class, emotions that originate elsewhere. Although he recognized that he'd "crossed the line," Professor Talcott Garland was unable to redeem himself.

Mark remembers a Talcott Garland incident from a recent Ethics class. The class was conducted primarily through small group and plenary discussion. During a plenary in which the class was exploring an issue that had been discussed in groups, Mark asked the class a question, the content of which he doesn't remember. A male student in the back row volunteered and began: "To play the Devil's Advocate …" Mark immediately responded, "You like to do that." The student had missed several classes, and when he was there, Mark had experienced his responses as aggressive, as if he had decided he wasn't going to go along with anything Mark or his peers suggested.

4 · WHO ARE OUR STUDENTS?   121

Mark sensed immediately that his comment wasn't appropriate, but wasn't sure what to do and consequently, went on with the class. Back in his office, he was concerned how his response had affected the student and how it had affected the rest of the class; even possibly, how it had affected the atmosphere in the classroom and subsequently, the course. The student had what seemed to Mark a Muslim name, and he wondered whether his judgment of the student had been partially shaped by his response to the name.

He spoke with Jean about the incident and resolved either to email the class or to speak about it in the following class a week later. He would think about what to say.

Shortly after that, the student appeared at Mark's door to speak with him about how inappropriate he'd felt the comment to be and how singled out he'd felt. Mark immediately acknowledged that he was "out of line" and apologized. They spoke for several minutes, and as the student left, Mark wasn't sure he'd been satisfied with Mark's response. Mark also wasn't satisfied; he wondered whether by responding so quickly with an apology, he'd shut down the student's opportunity to fully express his feelings.

Mark subsequently spoke to the class about the incident, although he couldn't determine whether speaking about it had alleviated any tension that might have developed from the encounter, not even whether most of the students had noticed it when it occurred. He never did resolve any of those questions and remained concerned for the remainder of the term. He also remains unsure how much that concern might have shaped his behavior during the remaining classes but suspects he became excessively cautious.

Mark and Professor Garland offer glimpses of how nightmare scenarios might feel to us; do they resonate? Many of us probably are familiar with the feelings of inadequacy that caused Martha Beck's entire Harvard classroom, including the teachers, to fake it. Perhaps, as Professor Christine Overall describes it, we feel like imposters, frauds.

In Mary McCarthy's novel *The Groves of Academe*, one of the characters, Howard Furness, believes the academic world is divided into three groups. He calls these groups

122   4 · WHO ARE OUR STUDENTS?

the "admitted frauds, [the] hypocritical frauds, [and the] unconscious frauds." "[T]his fraudulence," says McCarthy, "in fact, to [Howard's] glazed-pottery-blue eye, constituted the human."

As an academic I often feel I should align myself with the first category, the admitted frauds. The term captures a deep uneasiness at the heart of my experience as an academic. I even fantasize about opening a special chapter of Frauds Anonymous for university instructors: "I am Professor X and I am a fraud." For when I teach, I suffer from the imposter syndrome.[10]

And that may cause us to overcompensate, even to act foolishly.

Not only do we occasionally feel fraudulent; many of us also suffer under what Don Finkel and Stephen Monk call "The Atlas Complex,"[11] the feeling that we need to hold up the entire world on our shoulders, that without us doing everything, our students will learn nothing. And for some of us, the first even may lead to the second.

Consider the pervasive expression "I need to cover this material." The implication is that unless I do, something terrible will happen to my students. Such a dominant metaphor; who of us hasn't used it more than several times. Yet, for an academic institution, it's an (unintentionally?) ironic metaphor. More appropriate might be its opposite: *un*covering material. Or if we're thinking about learning, even better might be: working with our students to uncover ...

Not wanting to be Atlas, Mary Rose O'Reilley suggests that "[s]tudents do not listen well to the answers to questions they have not learned to ask."[12] That's often been our experience. Has it been yours?

However, if a person is convinced she's a fraud and is dominated by fear of failing or looking stupid, will they credit O'Reilley's suggestion? Will they ever learn to ask questions important to their learning? If we think they might not, how can we help create the conditions that won't lead to experiences like those in Professor Garland's classroom, conditions that will support rather than impede learning? We have several suggestions and hope you might add your own.

IV. What Can We Do to Facilitate Learning?

Here are several strategies we think could facilitate your students' learning. Most you've already seen in other contexts.

A. Teach Non-judgmentally/Teach Non-judgment

We have discussed teaching non-judgmentally extensively in Chapter 2, and by implication suggested that by modeling non-judgment, we also encourage our students to practice it. As much as we might be inclined to judge our students, they often seem even harsher on their peers than we are.

The three strategies suggested here and explained earlier model what it can mean to suspend judgment, and how, rather than constricting a person's horizons, they can expand them.

1. Employ (and encourage) Parallel Universe Thinking

2. Play the Believing Game

Similarly, by revealing more about each person, activities such as the "Thing of Beauty"[13] make people more appreciative of their peers. Seeing their peers' strengths, imaginative capacities, as well as the depth and breadth of their interests, students are less inclined to form quick negative judgments about them.

3. Lock Up Our Internal Critics (and encourage our students to lock up theirs)

To begin her wonderful book about writing,[14] poet, novelist, and writing teacher Natalie Goldberg offers her "Rules for Writing Practice." Her first rule is "Keep your hand moving." Here's how she explains it.

1. *Keep your hand moving.* When you sit down to write, whether it's for ten minutes or an hour, don't stop. If an atom bomb drops at your feet eight minutes after you've begun and you were going to write for ten minutes, don't budge. You'll go out writing.

What is the purpose of this? Most of the time, when we write, we mix up the editor and the creator. Imagine your writing hand as the creator and the other hand as the editor. Now bring your two hands together and lock your fingers. This is what happens when we write. The writing hand wants to write about what she did last Saturday night: "I drank whiskey all night and stared at a man's back across the bar. He was wearing a red T-shirt. I imagined him to have the face of Harry Belafonte. At three a.m., he finally turned my way and I spit into the ashtray when I saw him. He had the face of a wet mongrel who had lost his teeth." The writing hand is three words into writing this first sentence— "I drank whiskey ..."—when the other hand clenches her fingers tighter and the writing hand can't budge. The editor says to the creator, "Now that's not nice, the whiskey and stuff. Don't let people know that. I have a better idea: 'Last night, I had a nice cup of warmed milk and then went to bed a nine o'clock.' Write that. Go ahead. I'll loosen my grip so you can."[15]

Sound familiar? To us it does. We think most of us have powerful internal critics, telling us what *not* to say, telling us not to risk making mistakes. Think of some lawyers, who, in letters to clients, are gifted in saying very little while making it look as if they were extremely knowledgeable.

If that's true for us, it's doubly so for many of our students. For writers Goldberg offers several strategies, for example: "*Lose control.* Say what you want to say. Don't worry if it's correct, polite, appropriate."[16] "*Be specific.* Not car, but Cadillac. Not fruit, but apple. Not bird, but wren. Not a codependent, neurotic man, but Harry, who runs to open the refrigerator door for his wife, thinking she wants an apple, when she is headed for the gas stove to light her cigarette."[17] "*Go for the jugular.* If something scary comes up, go for it. That's where the energy is. Otherwise, you'll spend all your time writing around whatever makes you nervous. It will probably be abstract, bland writing because you're avoiding the truth."[18]

Even when someone isn't writing, several of these strategies might work. Can you think of others that might work for you and for your students?

B. Discern the Gift, Not the Gifted

As Mary Rose O'Reilley writes, so much of academic life is focused on identifying the most "gifted" students, separating the sheep from the goats. Yet typically, assessment methods are so narrowly drawn that many gifted students are ignored. Since we're so preoccupied with judging, we don't have time for the more expansive, and we think, much richer and more important goals of helping each student identify their gifts and then celebrating them. Ignoring that risks sending many promising people into the world discouraged and lacking self-confidence.

Take a minute and think of experiences that have made you doubt yourself, lose confidence. Try for detail: where you were, what was happening, what were the factors that contributed? Jot that down. Then do the same for moments when you felt your confidence increase, when you said to yourself, yes, I can do this. Does this process lead you to any thoughts about how you might facilitate a more positive learning experience for your students?

Of course, what discouraged and encouraged you may not be what does the same to any student. Do you think asking your class to perform a similar thought experiment might help them? If you facilitated one, would you want to know what they discovered? Would that help you improve your teaching?

Even if you didn't think it useful to work with an entire class, could this process work with a student who has come to your office, expressing doubts about himself?

C. Use Midstream, or Formative, Assessment

Discover how your students are (or aren't) learning. Too often we discover what our students learned and how they've experienced a course only after it's finished. And even then, we don't learn much. Course evaluations usually are like votes on a television game show; we see the boo and hooray meter, but little else. In many courses, work that students submit and we assess arrives as a finished product (usually at the end of a course), when it's too late for us or our students to revise their practices.

126   4 · WHO ARE OUR STUDENTS?

Rather than wait until the course is over or almost over, you can assess formatively, not to evaluate your or your students' performance, but to improve it.* You can use simple brief questions, say, asking your class before they leave to spend a minute or two thinking about a question, such as: "what's the most important/ confusing/challenging aspect of today's (this week's) class?" Ask them to jot down their responses and hand them to you as they leave. After learning how they're doing, you might be able to adjust your teaching accordingly.

Or you can design a longer, more detailed assessment. Here's one example. Around the end of the first third of your course, you identify a colleague whom you think would be helpful and willing to participate. She needn't be from your department; since she won't know your students and possibly, many of your colleagues, it might even be preferable for her not to be. The colleague first interviews you to discover what you're concerned about in the course, what you want to learn. After that, she'll meet with your class.

On the designated day, you introduce the colleague to your class and announce that she'll be conducting a learning assessment with them to see how things are going in the course: what's working, what could be improved. You promise that all individual comments will be kept confidential, that your colleague will report only the *results* of the assessment. You leave the room.

The colleague explains the procedure, again promising confidentiality. She asks the class to form into groups of 5 or 6, and asks each group to formulate a group response to 3 questions. Examples might be: What's working well in the course; what isn't working well; what might help the course become more effective? She asks each group to choose a reporter to record and report their responses.

Students discuss the questions in their groups, formulate a group answer, and each group's reporter reports. Your colleague

---

* In smaller seminars and case work, Jean uses a mid-semester evaluation format, in which she sits down one on one with students to discuss midcourse corrections for the course and supervision, and gives feedback on her student's professional development.

(or the group reporters) record their responses in a form that will allow her to take them back to you. During each report, or if she prefers, after all are finished, your colleague can encourage discussion. Since student perspectives are likely to be divergent, there probably will be considerable discussion.

Since the reporter is speaking for a group, not for herself, students are likely to be honest in their responses. No one need fear that Professor Garland will be able to identify a source.

After she thinks there's been ample discussion, your colleague leaves, reflects on the conversation, and brings you the assessment and her reflections. You discuss them with her, consider what you might be able to do to enhance what's working and improve what isn't, and report back to the class soon afterwards.

While useful, this process will use considerable class time. If you're unable to commit that time, consider using an expanded "one minute paper" session at the beginning or end of a class to ask the students to respond to the questions individually. While this truncated process lacks the extended group discussion of the more extensive one, you'll still receive valuable information.

With these examples, as well as in the brief one minute paper responses described above, reporting back is crucial. It tells students you're listening to them, allows them to feel that their learning experience matters to you, and that you're flexible enough to adapt. It builds community. And if the groups differ in their responses, it helps students appreciate that others may experience their learning from a perspective unlike their own and realize that to reach all students, teachers must respond to several learning styles and interests.

To report back does not require you to accept all suggestions. But for those you feel unable or unwilling to accept, you can explain why you're not implementing them. In most cases, students will understand your reasons and appreciate your willingness to explain.

D. Anticipate Difficult Incidents

Many teachers observe that problems they face in the classroom or teaching have happened before. A teacher could reflect on a dif-

128   4 · WHO ARE OUR STUDENTS?

ficult moment right after it occurs, or plan a reflection event around recurrent, dreaded awkward times in class.

The University of Victoria has developed a useful set of video-tapes showing critical incidents that might occur during any teaching experience and helping viewers reflect on possible responses to those incidents.[19]

E. Take One More Minute

Consider one habit we associate with our friend Gerry Hess, of the Gonzaga Law School-based Institute for Law Teaching and Learning.* Whenever a student approaches him about any topic, he generally asks something like: "So how's it going otherwise?" Imagine what someone like Gerry might have learned from Tanya Munro or Lisa Fong. Even a small investment of time could offer the student some support at a key moment. A regular habit of showing interest in students can perform a message of respect and genuine interest, which in turn, might help a student treat herself similarly.

This is now a reflex, which reminds us and our students that we care about each student beyond the presenting question. And we're often surprised; as often as we hear about sad or difficult trials, we often learn great news. "Thanks for asking; I just got engaged!"

Another way to take one more minute can occur in class. You might institutionalize a "Weather Report."** At the beginning or end of a class, invite students to proceed around the room describing their "weather." To some that might mean using meteorologist's terms: "sunny," "cloudy," "storm clouds gathering," etc. Or it might involve a student describing in more detail their current struggles with school work or with a parent or partner.

---

* Gerry reports that this is an adaptation of the "3-minute conversation he learned from Mark Levin, a participant at a teaching workshop at the University of Hawaii.

** We owe the term and the idea to Don Finkel.

F. Trust Ourselves

In *A Life in School*, Jane Tompkins writes that to become an effective teacher, she needed to learn to trust herself. "It was to my own experience that I needed to turn to for enlightenment."[20] Tompkins writes that her education failed to turn her attention to that experience, and consequently, that she didn't know, and didn't trust, herself.

Sometimes, when we do draw on our experience, our education chastises us for doing so.

Mark remembers such a time. When he was in his first year at law school, students were unhappy with their education, particularly with the Socratic method, the practice of which they found humiliating and demeaning. Being the late '60's, the students were vocal about their unhappiness. One professor, known for his liberal views, invited Mark and his roommate to write about their experience. Encouraged that he might get a sympathetic hearing, Mark did just that.

The teacher responded by letting Mark know that he thought Mark's responses were overblown, that there was no substance to them, in effect that Mark should stop grousing and get with the program. Feeling chastened, Mark became silent and tried to get with the program. It didn't work; during his remaining 2½ years, never felt comfortable and blamed himself as being inadequate to the study of law.

Several years later, the school initiated changes that were responsive to the earlier student complaints.

After becoming a teacher, it took ten years for Mark to find an authentic voice, one that felt grounded, one he trusted. For him, as for Tompkins, that's made all the difference, allowed him to risk more, to be more present to his students and to himself, and to occupy less space in the classroom.

V. Conclusion

Of course, not everyone acts out of fear, and no one constantly acts out of fear. Still, we do think that the judgmental dimensions of university education and our own self-critical faculties can, and regularly do, impede learning. For us, trusting ourselves, and trusting our students, can be antidotes to that fear, as we encourage our students to bring their best selves to our classrooms, to their relationships with us, with their peers, and with their subjects.

4 · WHO ARE OUR STUDENTS?

Notes

1. Mary Rose O'Reilley, *The Peaceable Classroom* (Portsmouth, NH: Boynton/Cook, 1993), 91.

2. Jane Tompkins, *A Life in School: What the Teacher Learned* (Reading, MA: Addison Wesley, 1996), 213.

3. Tanya Munro, "A Family's Criminal Legacy," *The Legal Studies Forum* 27 (2003): 403–405.

4. Stephanie Mah, "Gantarro Tower," *The Legal Studies Forum* 27 (2003): 371–73.

5. Lisa Fong, "*Sui Generis*," *The Legal Studies Forum* 27 (2003): 385–89.

6. Martha Beck, *Expecting Adam* (New York: Berkley Books, 1999), 76–78.

7. From *The Emperor of Ocean Park* by Stephen L. Carter, copyright © 2002. Used by permission of Alfred A. Knopf, a division of Random House, Inc.

8. Wayne C. Booth, *The Vocation of a Teacher: Rhetorical Occasions* (Chicago: The University of Chicago Press, 1988), 228–31.

9. Two wonderful stories exploring the implications of counter-transference are "Fat Lady" by psychiatrist Irvin D. Yalom in *Love's Executioner & Other Tales of Psychotherapy* (New York: Basic Books, 1989), a story about a psychiatrist who hates obese people but accepts an obese patient, and "Equitable Awards" by lawyer and novelist Louis Auchincloss in *Narcissa & Other Fables* (Boston: Houghton Mifflin Harcourt, 1983), a story about a middle aged woman wanting a divorce, who hires a younger female lawyer from a different generation with different values.

10. Christine Overall, *A Feminist I: Reflections from Academia* (Calgary: Broadview Press, 1998), 129.

11. Donald L. Finkel and G. Stephen Monk, "Dissolution of the Atlas Complex," in *Learning in Groups: New Directions for Teaching and Learning*, no. 14, eds. Clark Bouton and Russell Y. Garth (San Francisco: Jossey-Bass, 1983).

12. O'Reilley, *Peaceable Classroom*, 34.

13. See Chapter Five.

14. Natalie Goldberg, *Wild Mind: Living the Writer's Life* (New York: Bantam, 1990).

15. Ibid., 2.

16. Ibid., 3

17. Ibid.

18. Ibid., 4.

19. *Critical Incidents: Video Case Studies of Teaching Problems*. Victoria: University of Victoria Centre for Learning and Teaching, http://www.ltc.uvic.ca/servicesprograms/criticalincidents.

20. Tompkins, *Life in School*, xii.

Chapter 5

The Teacher and Vocation

[Teaching] is a profession that can seem, on a bad day, after a bad class, quite simply intolerable. "I've just got to get out of this, fast. I'll phone this afternoon to check into that early-retirement scheme." An hour later, a day later, the vocation can feel as fresh and rewarding as it did on that day long ago when I said, "All right, then, I'll be an English teacher, even though it does mean I'll always be poor." On the good days, I always find myself thinking what a coup it was to win all this and to be paid for it too.

—Wayne Booth,
The Vocation of a Teacher[1]

When we listen primarily to what we ought to be doing with our lives, we may find ourselves hounded by external expectations that can distort our identity and integrity … In contrast … Frederick Buechner offers a more generous and humane image of vocation as "the place where your deep gladness and the world's deep hunger meet."

In a culture that sometimes equates work with suffering, it is revolutionary to suggest that the best inward sign of vocation is deep gladness—revolutionary but true. If a work is mine to do, it will make me glad over the long haul, despite the difficult days … If a work does not gladden me in these ways, I need to consider laying it down.

—Parker Palmer,
The Courage to Teach[2]

What if you had nothing to prove? What if you undertook every class, every article, every meeting, every student and collegial in-

133

134   5 · THE TEACHER AND VOCATION

teraction, with no need or concern about proving anything to anyone? What would you be doing? Would you be living your teaching life as you now do? Would you write as you now write? Work as you now work? Maintain the same relationship between your professional and personal lives? To answer these questions would be to express what for you would be a life lived in vocation, a life unburdened by trying to fulfill the external expectations imposed, or that we imagine to be imposed, by others.

Yet many of us do find ourselves being governed from the outside, by fear of failing or looking foolish. We try too hard to please others; we measure our success by external standards. Here again is Wayne Booth, one of North America's most celebrated literary critics and an award winning teacher:

> Among my many character flaws—perhaps shared with many teachers (it led us into teaching?)—is an absurd insecurity, an obsessive need to be loved and approved by all. This leads to wasted energy, wasted emotion, unwise acceptance of tasks to which I am unsuited. And it often leads to grotesque errors of judgment, some of which can sear my memory for decades.[3]

For many of us, these barriers to living in vocation persist throughout our lives.

In this Chapter we invite you to explore what it might mean to live and work without these barriers. And to explore these questions in a way that's tailored to meet your individual needs. We'll focus first, on vocation writ large, its substance and processes, and then will explore several specific dimensions of a teacher's vocation. We've divided the Chapter into three sections: *Discovering Vocation, Nurturing Vocation,* and *Some Elements of a Teacher's Vocation.* In each section you'll find a mixture of exercises, stories, critical incidents, and attempts to capture the meaning of vocation. We hope they'll help you identify or clarify your vocation and help you sustain it, as well as nurture it in others.

I. Discovering Vocation

A. Understanding Vocation

Poem Postcard

*I would have written you a letter instead of a postcard, but
I didn't have time.
I wanted to tell you about what was happening in my life,
but I didn't have time.
I would have invited you to dinner, but I didn't have time.
I would have done more reading before writing this paper,
but I didn't have time.
We never got to cover the end of the novel because we ran
out of time.
I would have read your article more carefully, but I didn't
have time.
I didn't have time to read your article,
I wanted to call you, but I was afraid it would take too much
time.*

In haste, Jane[4]

Does this poem postcard express how you often feel: rushed, scattered, constantly interrupted, so busy you're unable to do what you most want to do? Perhaps that's why you picked up this book: to find a guide for slowing down, integrating the different dimensions of your life? Or perhaps, confirming what Wayne Booth suggests most of us feel periodically, you've recently experienced one of those discouraging moments or periods when you wonder if you're in the right profession, wonder if your vocation lies elsewhere?

What *does* it mean to lead a life in vocation? Theologian Frederick Buechner understands vocation to be that "place where your deep gladness and the world's deep hunger meet."[5] Let's explore briefly each of the three elements in Buechner's conception, after which we'll turn to our own conceptions.

Your Deep Gladness: The Call of the True Self

For each of us, our deep gladness, that which gives us abiding, profound joy, is the call of our true self. In a society where our time schedules are like the ones described in Jane Tompkins's postcard poem, pressing us to look for a quick fix, the call of our deep gladness invites us to look elsewhere, within ourselves. To look within ourselves, to our identity, or core, implies that when we find our deep gladness, it will sustain us in both good times and bad. In that way, it differs from happiness. The joy of deep gladness does not depend on us enjoying good luck, or on good times or smooth sailing. This is the joy that keeps us grounded, content, at peace with ourselves, even in turbulent times.

Joy is self-validating. Joy also can be mystifying. We may not know why we find it so enjoyable to play tennis, put together a jigsaw puzzle, or bake a loaf of bread, or why the sight of a beautiful painting in a museum, or the sound of our favorite music on the radio lightens our heart, even on the most difficult day. But these examples suggest the joy we're describing and inviting you to identify. The joy that is not located in any single moment or particular context, that motivates you today as it did ten years ago, and as you have reason to believe, will continue to do so ten years from now.

The World's Deep Hunger: Which Call? Whose Call?

The call of the world's deep hunger is vast and multi-vocal. For each of us to try to answer its many voices is impossible. So, as we invite you to identify what that call is for you, we're also inviting you to give yourself permission not to answer all the calls that you hear.

How would you encapsulate what for you is the call of the world's deep hunger? For lawyers we might think of it as the call of justice. For doctors, would it be the call of healing? For artists, the call of beauty?

Teachers hear many calls—calls from their subject matter, calls from their educational mission. What speaks to you: the call of understanding, or discovery? the call of learning? the call of your discipline? Take a moment to consider how you would summarize, in a word or phrase, the call(s) that most compel you.

Here's Jean on a moment of hearing her call.

5 · THE TEACHER AND VOCATION

Jean recently had read an exercise challenging her to summarize her mission statement in a bumper sticker, which seemed a preposterous task. While ridiculing the exercise to her children one afternoon in the car, a word came to her: "*Home.*" At the time, Jean was a clinical teacher, who, with her students, was representing parents, children, and refugees in a law school legal services organization; she also was the mother of two children, then 9 and 6.

Jean wondered aloud to her children whether she had just received a clue that maybe her motto for what she cared about in life was "Home." And, she continued, that motto makes sense: "What do I do? I represent refugees. Who are they? They're people pulled from their homes, trying to find a new home in the United States. I represent children. What children? Children who are removed from their homes. I represent parents. What parents? Parents whose children are taken from their homes. Maybe 'Home' *is* my motto."

"But Mommy, if that was your motto, you would be home all the time."

To which her other child replied, "Wait a minute, maybe what she's saying is the only thing that would take her from our home is to help someone else find *their* home."

Have you had an experience like this one? Is there a word, a phrase, a quotation, an image, that encapsulates *your* call? Sit with this question for a while and see what comes up.

In addition to finding your call, we also ask you to identify those calls of the world's deep hunger that you cannot answer, and to forgive yourself for not trying to answer them. In our media saturated times, doing this can be difficult. What are the calls you constantly hear that tear at your heart but cannot be answered now? For many of us who have revered the medical profession but lacked all of the skills required for this call, we must let go of the aspiration of being a great surgeon, or curing AIDS or breast cancer. Or those of us who loved writing stories when we were young may not be able to become the next Alice Munro. Sorting through the calls of the world's deep hunger is a constant challenge, but no challenge is greater than that of daring to hear the sounds of the

138   5 · THE TEACHER AND VOCATION

world's calls as you search for the ones you can authentically answer.

In fact, your gladness may help you hear the call more clearly. In this information age, we worry less that the call of the world's deepest hunger will reach you, and more that the cacophony of anguish will overwhelm or numb you. Joy's ear may help you tune in to the cries you can hear and answer best.

<u>Where Deep Gladness and the World's
Deep Hunger Meet: An Illustration</u>

Do you remember why Luke Skywalker in the first *Star Wars* movie was able to destroy the Death Star through a thermal exhaust port only 2 meters wide? He'd been doing (and enjoying) it for years. "I used to bull's-eye womp rats in my T-16 back home. They're not much bigger than 2 meters!" And when the deed was begun, what did Luke whoop? "It'll be just like Beggar's Canyon back home."

What is your Beggar's Canyon? The path of vocation requires you to recover and experience your deepest joy, daily, and to offer it in service of the calls that move you most—justice, healing, understanding, beauty, learning—whatever you designate. And the aim of delighting in the service of the most compelling may evolve for you, as it has for some of us, from a quest for identity—Who am I?—to a quest in faith—Whose am I? Our musings on vocation quickly implicate our deepest beliefs, our spirituality, and, for some, our relationship to the Divine.

B. Finding Your Vocation: Four Exercises

What follows are four exercises that might help you identify, understand, and possibly, more thoroughly embrace, your vocation. Try one or two and see where they take you.

1. *Write Your Obituary*

One way to discover your path might be to begin at the end and explore what you'd want said about you at the end of your life. Take some time with your journal and compose either your obituary or a eulogy for your funeral. If they help, use the following guidelines:

5 · THE TEACHER AND VOCATION

a.) don't fret about any detail (which newspaper, what length, the identity of the author, the date of the article or speech) unless it sparks your creativity. If a choice of detail blocks you, choose the least anxiety-provoking alternative and keep writing;

b.) beyond grounding the basic facts in reality, feel free at any point to reach into imagination or fantasy;

c.) if you get stuck, observe what stimulates your writing and also what impeded it, and go back to a;

d.) hang in there. When you're finished, explore whether you've found some meaning in your life independent of the need to have proven yourself to the world.*

---

* Here is an example of each, composed by Sophie Sparrow, one of the participants at the 2003 *Reflecting on Our Teaching* retreat, held in Leavenworth, Washington.

Obituary

[Name] died last week at the age of eighty-two. The mother of two children, [name] 50, of Vancouver, and [name], 48 of San Francisco and Hawaii, she was the wife of [name], who predeceased her by three years. The deceased taught law students and wrote about the art of teaching. She was a professor and dean, but is most widely recognized for her work on writing and teaching about teaching.

But perhaps her most important source of recognition is as the mother of her 2 children. Her daughter, [name], noted author, writer, teacher, artist and performer and her son, [name], the performer/designer, have both made a name for themselves individually and as collaborators. Her son has designed a new jet, plays rhythm guitar, and designs play spaces for adults. Her daughter teaches students from the Kindergarten to graduate level, leads retreats, designs clothing and furniture, writes novels, and consults on leadership issues. In addition to their individual contributions, together they design space, lead retreats where adults return to their play selves, and also conduct workshops on raising friendly siblings and addressing sibling rivalry/partnership. Together the deceased's children have co-authored several books and are currently going on a world tour/leadership consulting trip that will take them to Singapore, Malaysia, India, China, Mongolia, Nigeria, Kenya, Australia, New Zealand, and Europe.

140   5 · THE TEACHER AND VOCATION

2. *Find and Explore a Governing Metaphor*

As a way into "the mystery of our selfhood," Parker Palmer invites us to fill in the blank in the following sentence: "When I am teaching at my best, I am like a _____."[6] He suggests you "accept the image that arises, resisting the temptation to censor or edit it."[7] To illustrate the "risk and payoff" of this mode of self-understanding, Palmer offers his own metaphor.

> ... [W]hen I am teaching at my best, I am like a sheepdog—not the large, shaggy, loveable kind, but the all-business Border Collies one sees working the flocks in sheep country.
>
> ...
>
> In my imagination—unfettered by expert knowledge of the real thing—the sheepdog has four vital functions.

Eulogy

From my daughter:

Mom was mom. She was a real mom. When we were younger, we used to criticize her for not being a real mom. She wasn't real when she was busy, distracted, focused on work, tired, cranky and dressed in work clothes. A real mom wore faded jeans, cotton hooded sweatshirts, and faded worn shirts. That was mom.

She didn't often make cookies and stay home so we could see her after school, but she was real. Mom made us think, *why?* "Why did what I just did make you mad?" She'd ask. "How can I be a better mom?" "[Name], how can I keep from procrastinating?" She honored us by treating us like her collaborators. We weren't her chummy buddies in the sense that we ever forgot who was the parent, but we collaborated in family dynamic improvements. When we'd complain or be upset, or have a bad vacation, she always got us to reflect. "So, how can you make it better? How could it be different? What is it that made that special?"

She gave us the gift of knowing ourselves. Of listening. Of developing a voice. Of thinking/doubting/believing. She gave us the joy of growth. She knew she wouldn't physically be with us, but she gave us the tools to always keep her in our souls. She encouraged us to grow, to fly, to soar. We have. Thanks Mom.

5 · THE TEACHER AND VOCATION

It maintains a space where the sheep can graze and feed themselves; it holds sheep together in that space, constantly bringing back strays; it protects the boundaries of that space to keep dangerous predators out; and when the grazing ground is depleted, it moves with the sheep to another space where they can get the food they need.

It is obvious, I suppose, where I am going with all this, though when I began exploring the image it was not obvious to me. From the crude and uncomfortable image of myself as a sheepdog, I evolved a more refined image of teaching ...: to teach is to create a space in which the community of truth can be served.

My task in the classroom, I came to see, parallels this imaginative rendering of the sheepdog's task. My students must feed themselves—that is called active learning. If they are to do so, I must take them to a place where food is available: a good text, a well-planned exercise, a generative question, a disciplined conversation. Then, when they have learned what there is to learn in that place, I must move them to the next feeding ground. I must hold the group within those places, paying special attention to those individuals who get lost or run away—and all the while I must protect the group from deadly predators, like fear.[8]

Once you've finished exploring your metaphor, why not invite several colleagues to do the same and then meet to share what you've discovered? That could offer everyone imaginative fuel for discussing how we teach and learn, together with an appreciation for a variety of teaching styles.

3. *Compose a Job Description*

In her thoughtful and provocative book, Radical *Presence: Teaching as Contemplative Practice*, Mary Rose O'Reilley describes returning to teaching from a sabbatical in a Quaker community and finding that it "had pretty much unfitted me for the academic world I had left behind ... I was no longer able to tell my students

142   5 · THE TEACHER AND VOCATION

what they needed to know, because I didn't know what they needed to know, though only a year ago, I had been quite sure."[9]

Despairing about being able to do her job, even to know what her job required of her, O'Reilley asked herself a question that echoed what her spiritual director had been asking her in her Quaker community. *"What are you doing? What are you really doing? What is your deepest sense of call? Your true vocation?"*[10] She decided to compose a job description, to "write down a sentence that reflected my clearest sense of the task."[11] O'Reilley wrote *"Peaceful listening ...* The only thing that needs to happen is peaceful listening."

We think O'Reilley's question is a wonderful one, worth trying to answer for yourself. Here's how in a recent essay Mark responded to her question.

> I like O'Reilley's response and could adopt it for my own. It's certainly become a central part of my self-understanding as a teacher. But if I were to respond to O'Reilley's question today, I'd choose as my job description: *Giving permission*, or better, encouraging my students to give themselves permission. Permission to bring yourself to your work, to step forward, to risk being present in what you write and what you say. Permission to care. Permission to take your classmates and yourself seriously: as writers, as thinkers, as individuals responsible for the shape of the law. Permission to set your own goals and see what it might mean to work toward accomplishing them.
>
> When in my [Legal Imagination] course students have taken that permission, I've been rewarded, we've been rewarded, with lively, funny, provocative, thoughtful, humane essays, deeply reflective about the law and about each individual's place in it, and with similarly lively, provocative classroom conversations. They've confirmed me in believing that it's worth taking the time to try to listen and respond to each voice as it presents itself. To be heard, or seen, can be a profoundly moving experience:

5 · THE TEACHER AND VOCATION   143

affirming, encouraging, sometimes leading to dramatic, and positive life changes.[12]

Try composing your own job description, your clearest sense of your task. Not the task that someone or some institution has imposed on you, but the one you'd choose if you had nothing to prove. How does it compare to the one your institution or department head would write? If they differ, can you imagine doing your job as you've described it for yourself? What would change from how you now work? What would remain?

4. *Visit or Write Your Future Self*

The following meditation by Karen Saakvitne and Laurie Pearlman invites you, through guided imagery, to an encounter with your future self. To transition to the guided imagery, you may want to start with a few minutes of quiet breathing or meditation. If you want to stay with your eyes closed during the meditation, consider taping it, with pauses after each sentence, and using the tape in a quiet moment.

> Imagine entering your future self's office or work space. As your future self welcomes you, look around. What do you notice about the space? What object do you see? What do you notice about your future self? What do you look like? How have you changed, grown, and matured? Take some time and notice the feelings you have in the room. Breathe in the air, and take the opportunity now to find a place to sit opposite or beside your future self. Feel your body supported in the seat you have chosen. Notice the temperature in the room. Look at the light and colors; notice any smells.

Listen now as you and your future self converse about your work life. Are there any questions you wish to ask your future self? Go ahead and ask those now … And listen to your future self's thoughtful response. How does your future self feel about the work? What is most rewarding? What are some proudest memories? What is most comforting? (Pause—5 mins.)

How does your future self feel at the end of the day of work? Listen and ask any questions that come to mind. (Pause)

Is there anything your future self would like to ask you? Anything she or he wants to tell or suggest to you, or to give to you? (Pause—5 mins.)

Although only a short amount of clock time has elapsed, you can sense that you have had all the time you need for now with your future self. Your time together is almost complete and your future self invites you to bring back with you anything you wish. Is there something in the office, some aspect or object, that will help you remain connected to your future self? You may pick it out and take it back to the present with you. (Pause)

It is time to say goodbye. (Stand at door.) You know you will meet at some future point.[13]

At our last retreat, several participants saw powerful images in this meditation—of their office door and themselves. One got a clear answer to a current vocational dilemma. Others preferred to ponder their experience privately. What is *your* experience?

We have also benefitted from writing letters to ourselves, written in a lucid moment or a moment of transition to yourself at a fixed point in the future. Jean and her family attend the summer Northfield conference, where letters are collected to be sent back on Valentine's Day; the conference calls them "Roses in Winter." Have a friend or officemate keep it and send it to you. It can remind you of deep commitments and insights over time.

C. A Life Lived in Vocation: Implications

When we speak of our professional life, we tend to frame that conversation in terms of a career. By contrast, Christian theologian James Fowler suggests that framing our life in terms of vocation would radically reorient our self-understanding.[14] Fowler offers seven consequences of living a life in vocation instead of a life in career. In the following chart we've juxtaposed Fowler's views on a life in vocation to a life focused on career:

5 · THE TEACHER AND VOCATION

From Career to Vocation: A Paradigm Shift

CAREER Who am I? What's in teaching for me?	VOCATION Whose am I? Who am I in teaching for? (James Fowler)
Vindicating our Worth through Achievement	*Nothing to Prove*
Success is zero sum, won through competition, over the defeat of others. Other talented, like-minded people are our rivals for scarce resources, jobs, prestige.	1. Called to an excellence that is not based on competition with others. Called to a vocational adventure that is distinct from that of anyone else.
	2. Freed from anxiety about whether someone else will beat us to that singular achievement that would have justified our lives.
	3. Freed to rejoice in the gifts and graces of others. In vocation we are augmented by others' talents rather than being diminished or threatened by them. An ecology of giftedness.
Seeking skill, talent, opportunity, money; "dying with our options open"; limits are frustrating, must be overcome.	4. Freed from jealousy and envy, we are freed from the sense of having to be all things to all people. In vocation we can experience our limits as gracious, even as we can experience our gifts as gracious.
Work and home are separate; work comes first. Maximize billable hours.	5. Freed to seek a responsible balance in the investment of our time and energy. Vocation is the opposite of workaholism (vocation encompasses career and home, daily life).
Time is our enemy—too much work, too little time.	6. Freed from the tyranny of time. Time is our friend.
Personal life is straightforward, shouldn't interfere with work.	7. Freed to see vocation as dynamic, as changing its focus and pattern over time, while continuing as a constant intensifying calling.

146   5 · THE TEACHER AND VOCATION

In universities we tend to measure our successes comparatively. Our differential salaries reflect judgments of our "merit." We compete against each other for a fixed pool of financial resources. We measure ourselves by our success at being published in the most prestigious journals. And we pass that competitiveness on to our students. As Mary Rose O'Reilley puts it: "[T]hat's what teaching *should* be about ... discerning the gift. Too often, by contrast, the central discipline of our craft is judging."[15] We discern the gifted, not the gift.

In vocation, since we have nothing to prove, and since each vocation is unique, we aren't competing with each other. Everyone is following their own path, a path they have no need to justify. Consequently, rather than ranking ourselves and others, we're free to recognize, enjoy, root for and feel enriched by each person's gifts.

In a world of infinite gifts, we "are freed from the sense of having to be all things to all people."[16] No more trying to be Atlas.[17] Instead, we can welcome, even embrace, our limits, as well as our own gifts.

"We are freed to seek a responsible balance in the investment of our time and energy."[18] In vocation we aren't workaholics. Rather than enforce a rigid separation between our professional and personal lives, a life in vocation can be an integrated life.

Living in vocation, we change our conception of time. Consider this postcard.

Postcard from the Edge

Dear C.,

Do you remember once we were having a telephone conversation about how busy we were? You were worrying about how you were ever going to finish that critical biography you'd been working on like a dog for years. We'd been talking about our families, when suddenly you burst out with: "I don't know what I would do. If my parents should die I wouldn't have time."
I'll never forget that moment, or the sound of your voice.

Jane[19]

Unlike life for the author of this postcard and the one beginning this section, for whom time is a tyrant, in vocation, time can be our friend. With nothing to prove, we can let go of some of the "shoulds" that devour our time.*

Finally, our vocation is dynamic. As we grow and develop, so will our vocation. While remaining a constant calling, its shape and textures may change, reflecting the changing patterns in our lives.

II. Nurturing Vocation in Ordinary Times: Two Sets of Processes You Can Trust

There is a profound connection between the large lifetime issues of vocation we've been exploring and the routines of daily life. Vocation calls us to live our lives in this moment. An event like September 11, 2001, can make us starkly aware how important it can be to live each moment fully; after that day, many of us were asking ourselves: if I were to die today, would I be doing what I am meant to be doing? Vocation promises that consistently focusing on the present will eventually add up to a life's work, because *how we spend our days is, of course, how we spend our lives.*[20]

How best can we be engaged every day nurturing and executing our vocation? To help us do that, we might use what we call "daily processes you can trust." We've identified two sets of these processes. The first set is internal, involving daily practices that help a vocation seeker focus without outside interference on her deep gladness, her concerns about world's deep hunger, and the place where they meet. In this process you can trust, your internal voices are strengthened and heard regularly, separate from the external voices, which tend to drown out internal messages.

---

* Of course, we can't ignore them all; as university teachers, we have obligations that define our work, obligations we must fulfill, no matter how distasteful. However, this chapter urges you to consider how seriously those obligations interfere with your deep gladness and to eliminate as many as possible from your day. For those that remain, as you respond to them, we encourage you to use only processes you can trust.

148   5 · THE TEACHER AND VOCATION

In the external processes you can trust, a vocation seeker takes action in the world and uses time-tested methods for planning her work, interacting with others, teaching her students, pursuing her scholarship, and attending to her chosen path. While the first process requires engagement with the self, the second requires engagement with the world.

Franklin Delano Roosevelt provides a fascinating study in both processes you can trust. An extremely gregarious man, he organized his actions in the world around social gatherings, having a daily cocktail hour with intimate friends and housing close friends in the White House for years at a time. He clearly was a man capable of extremely hard work, as his twelve years in office during the most turbulent times of American history demonstrated. And yet, at one critical moment during the war years with England, he just stopped working.

It is 1940, and Britain, trying to stave off German victory at sea, is desperate for American help. Two things are clear: Britain can't do it alone, and despite Roosevelt's sympathy, the United States Congress and much of its population are unwilling to enter this war. Although the situation is dire, Roosevelt decides to go on a ten-day Caribbean sail on a navy cruiser. On the first days he fishes and enjoys his leisure in the company of his friends. One evening, after receiving a letter from Winston Churchill, he has a vision: Lend-Lease, or the lending of war supplies, including aircraft and land vehicles, to Allied Forces. In his fireside chat, several days later, Roosevelt explains the concept:

> Suppose my neighbor's home catches on fire, and I have a length of garden hose four or five hundred feet away. If he can take my garden hose and connect it up with his hydrant, I may help to put out his fire. Now what do I do? I don't say to him before that operation, "Neighbor, my garden hose cost me $15—I want $15 for it." What is the transaction that goes on? I don't want $15— I want my garden hose back after the fire is over. All right. If it goes through the fire all right, intact, without any damage to it, he gives it back to me and thanks me very

5 · THE TEACHER AND VOCATION   149

much for the use of it. Of course, the neighbor would re-
place the hose if it couldn't be returned.

This was the concept of Lend-Lease, which Churchill hailed before Parliament as "the most unsordid act in the history of any na-
tion." [21] Many believed this decision was a turning point in World
War II.

The internal processes FDR could trust included withdrawing
from the scene of active work, deep rest, relaxation and meditative recreation, and the company of trusted friends. After many
days of these processes, he got the inspiration the world needed.
To introduce the idea to America, he resorted to a critical external process he could trust: the fireside chat, in which he explained his concept with a folksy metaphor accessible to all
Americans.

What are the processes *you* can trust? The next two segments
offer some questions you might consider as you identify your established, trusted processes.

A. Internal Processes You Can Trust

The internal processes you can trust focus on orientation: getting your bearings. In quiet solitude one asks: am I headed in the
right direction? Am I attuned to my own true instincts and de-
sires? In contrast to a life in the world, efficient, and constantly
pressed, during the internal process you can trust, you're trying
to be open-minded, open to inspiration, sensitive to messages
from within.

Here are several useful components for constructing and sustaining a process you can trust.

- Solitude or the company of an absolutely trustworthy companion;
- Sufficient time to enter a proactive state of thinking (perhaps,
  a minimum of 15 minutes?);
- A spirit of non-judgment towards oneself and a clear sense
  of nothing to prove;

5 · THE TEACHER AND VOCATION

- A meditative process—running, praying, meditating, yoga—any repetitive process that engages the entire mind.

In Chapter 2 we offered several suggestions for discovering or creating internal processes you can trust for your daily life:

1. *Investigate your daily routines.*
2. *Identify trustworthy interlocutors.*
3. *Identify the processes you can't trust.*
4. *Remember an inspired moment, and work backwards to recreate the processes that led to it.*

Here are several others.

5. *Consider adding processes to your day that complement your current routines.*

Looking at the whole of your daily activities—the balance of work and play, the balance of input (the reading, lectures, listening) and output (writing, lecturing, opining)—consider what is missing and how it might be added. For instance, if your examination of your daily routine shows that you spend many sedentary hours with others in dialogue, adding a short quiet solitary walk could enhance your process.

6. *Pay attention to clear, even if seemingly random, directives, past and present.*

Vocation often calls in the guise of serendipity, coincidence. Think of the way your career, and the careers of those around you, have evolved. Often, invitations to new paths come quietly, without fanfare. And although you may not know why, you feel you must take up that invitation. Jean remembers hearing an announcement in church in 1983, about the new asylum law and the need for lawyers to be trained in the field. At the time, she was a full time Legal Aid lawyer working with children, but something impelled her to go to the daylong training. She returned to her full time work, couldn't figure out how to incorporate her training, and forgot it. Until 1992, when her clinical teaching led her into asylum practice and teaching, which she continues to this day.

5 · THE TEACHER AND VOCATION

Similarly, Mark remembers seeing an announcement for the inaugural Canadian Law Teachers' Clinic, to be held in the spring of 1979. Always interested in teaching, and curious, but without any idea what shape the week-long Clinic would assume, he decided to attend. He could not have known that participating in the Clinic, re-experiencing himself there as a student, would lead him to radically revise his conception of himself as a teacher, to realize that in insisting on a fierce, argumentative style of conducting classes, he wasn't thinking of his students' needs, as he had told himself, but rather was driven by his fear of being inadequate, his need to "prove" to his students (and himself) that he knew what he was talking about.[22]

When seen in hindsight, clear, seemingly random directives sometimes turn out to be preparation in advance, as they did here. A call from a future time, if you will. Can you remember a clear, seemingly random directive that turned out to be preparation in advance? Are you hearing any clear, seemingly random directives now?

Here's one extended example from Canadian writer Wayson Choy. As a creative writing student at the University of British Columbia in 1958, Choy wrote a story that was published in the UBC journal *Prism*, and later anthologized in *Best American Stories for 1962*. His teachers encouraged him to continue writing, but he became discouraged, and feeling he had nothing to say, he stopped. He became an English teacher in Toronto. In 1977, his mother died, and he took a sabbatical to be with his father in Vancouver and to enroll again in UBC's Creative Writing program. Choy continues the story:

> … As luck would have it, Carol Shields was the no-nonsense short story instructor. She believed that if you were going to be a writer, you should be able to create a story from any source. For one assignment, she tore up pieces of paper, each marked with a colour, and set the rule: whichever colour you picked up, that colour had to become a major part of your next short story. I got pink.
>
> Unknown to me, my chance selection of pink turned out to be a sign. Let me explain about 'signs'. My immigrant parents were working all hours during my childhood in the 1940s, so I was partly raised by some of the last sur-

152   5 · THE TEACHER AND VOCATION

viving pioneers of Vancouver's Chinatown, the elders who originally sojourned from Old China villages. They imbued in me the folk wisdom of paying attention to signs; that is, to note events and coincidences that would prove meaningful to my fate. For example, I didn't know what picking up 'pink' might mean. I sensed the colour had some significance, but I was stuck. I walked into the kitchen where my two aunts and my father were mulling over my mother's pieces of jade. I overheard one of my aunts mention that as well as the usual green jade, there was pink jade. I left the kitchen. After about an hour, I walked back in and they were talking about the peony heads blooming in my aunt's garden. For some reason, the phrase 'jade peony' gripped me, and I immediately saw in my mind's eye an elderly hand shakily pressing an object of pink jade into a small boy's open palm. The first sentence came to me. That night, I typed out ... "When Grandmamma died at the age of 83, our family held its breath."

The story, "The Jade Peony," was one of two selected by Carol and my classmates to be submitted to the UBC Alumni Chronicle writing contest. It won, and the story was published a year later. I thought that would be the end of things, but the story appeared at a time when multicultural voices were gaining attention. "The Jade Peony" became a favorite of anthologies, and then, in 1992, Patsy Aldana at Douglas and McIntyre offered me a contract to write a book. Three years later, the novel *The Jade Peony*, was published. I'm amazed to think where my writing life would be today if, more than 25 years ago, Carol Shields hadn't challenged her students by tearing up those pieces of paper. Her no-nonsense ghost must be smiling.[23]

In the end, what do these processes yield? At their best, they can keep our eyes on the prize—orient, or reorient, us to vocation before we head back into the world to try to pursue that vocation. At least, they can help us regroup our energy, get quiet, hear our own thoughts, even regain our sense of humor.

B. External Processes You Can Trust

I arise in the morning torn between a desire to improve (or save) the world and a desire to enjoy (or savor) the world. This makes it hard to plan the day.
—*E. B. White*[24]

Using external processes you can trust to execute your vocation means that you need not choose between saving and savoring. At work, even with a clear sense of the day's or even our life's vocation, we must choose what processes we use to pursue that vocation. Here we are looking for a different set of processes: ones we can deeply enjoy and successfully use to muster our best working and interpersonal skills in service of our vocation. Explore which ones work best for you.

Consider the following exercise:

1. Make a list of all the different processes in your work day (meetings, class, labs, committee meetings, telephone calls, writing time, email correspondence, talks at the water cooler). Think about the way you spend your work day. Do you have days that are spent, say, entirely in meetings? Is the day you teach class a good day, or a dreaded one, or something else? Do you meet with students often? Seldom? Never? How is your writing time structured: in small bursts? In long reflective passages of time? Do you lunch with colleagues, or alone at your desk? Brainstorm the various ways you spend your work time. Challenge yourself to make the list as long and as complete as possible.

2. Circle the processes that you enjoy. If you enjoy some meetings, and not others, make a list of enjoyable ones and circle them.

3. Draw an X through the processes that you do not enjoy.

154   5 · THE TEACHER AND VOCATION

4. Once you have exhausted both lists, review your information, and look for trends. Are there clearly processes that work for you, that you can trust, and processes that clearly don't?

Consider Jean's recent experience as her vocation took an unusual turn. After eighteen years as a clinical law teacher, in which her classroom teaching took place exclusively in the context of representing clients in actual cases, Jean's internal processes she could trust led her to a clear, seemingly random directive. Jean had represented children in child protective proceedings for many years, and had written a book on the subject; at the time, she also was teaching a clinic at her law school, supervising students doing that work. As she completed a draft of an article on international developments in the field, developments that she had been unaware of until recently, she got a clear message during her journaling and prayer time: investigate how the countries of the world are assuring that children's voices are heard in child protective proceedings, and create a website with your global findings.

Although the reason for the message was not clear, the directive was strong enough that Jean decided to follow it. Doing so required her to teach her first non-clinical seminar, in which class discussion and supervision of major papers replaced one-on-two supervision of student work for clients. At first, she was terrified. However, excitement replaced terror whenever she had a new idea of how to teach in this new format. As part of the course she decided to hold individual meetings with her students; to help them write their papers, she organized a peer review process, which required students to work on their writing in teams; and to vary the learning formats in class, she used interactive classroom techniques. In each case, her "new" strategy was in fact an old one: exported from her clinical teaching, with which she was entirely comfortable, into this new, unfamiliar setting.

Just as vocation is born in gladness, it must grow through the gladness of a daily life. If you have always detested meetings, execute your vocation another way, through a process that you would love. Although most books are written in solitude, this one emerged through a process of collaboration between Mark and Jean that involved weekly telephone calls, readings that seemed off-topic, "aha" emails, voice recognition software, meetings with research assistants, presentations to groups, three retreats, as well as the hours at the word processor we usually associate with writing. Beware of hamstringing your vocation with processes that do not work for you.

III. Some Elements of a Teacher's Vocation

So far we have looked at a teacher's vocation writ large—its substance and its processes. Many of the strategies we've suggested for looking at the larger issue of your vocation as a teacher you also can apply to its differing dimensions. For instance, imagine that you're struggling with the question of how you should approach your university administrative duties (committee work, faculty meetings). Consider using a prompt you've found useful earlier—for example, reviewing high points and low points in your teaching—and extrapolating it to that specific dimension of your work. The exercise then would become: reflect on the high points and low points in your experience with administrative duties.

In addition to suggesting you adapt earlier prompts for reflecting, in this section we introduce the voices of several teachers describing how they have pursued their vocation in two dimensions of their teaching lives: writing and classroom teaching. What these teachers say and do probably diverges from standard practice, and you may find their words and actions provocative. They certainly represent distinctive perspectives. Whether you feel supported by the views expressed, challenged by them, or even hostile to them, we hope reflecting on them will help you clarify your own views about these dimensions of teaching. While we agree with many of the choices these teachers have made, in this section our goal is not to bludgeon you to agree, but rather to offer rich, detailed, provocative examples to prompt your reflection. However, if you don't find this strategy useful, please return to others more suited to your style.

156   5 · THE TEACHER AND VOCATION

A. Writing

As a writer, what if you had nothing to prove? Would you write your articles as you now do? Use the dispassionate, "objective" style favored in so many academic journals? Or would you prefer to be more present in what you write? Consider these excerpts from an essay by law professor Patricia Williams.[25] As you read, ask yourself whether you think they're appropriate for a journal article, which is how it first appeared. Is the essay an example of someone writing as if she had nothing to prove?

The Death of the Profane
(a commentary on the genre of legal writing)

Patricia J. Williams

Buzzers are big in New York City. Favored particularly by smaller stores and boutiques, merchants throughout the city have installed them as screening devices to reduce the incidence of robbery: if the face at the door looks desirable, the buzzer is pressed and the door is unlocked. If the face is that of an undesirable, the door stays locked. Predictably, the issue of undesirability has revealed itself to be a racial determination. While controversial enough at first, even civil-rights organizations backed down eventually in the face of arguments that the buzzer system is a "necessary evil," that it is a "mere inconvenience" in comparison to the risks of being murdered, that suffering discrimination is not as bad as being assaulted, and that in any event it is not all blacks who are barred, just 17-year-old black males wearing running shoes and hooded sweatshirts.

The installation of these buzzers happened swiftly in New York; stores that had always had their doors wide open suddenly became exclusive or received people by appointment only. I discovered them and their meaning one Saturday in 1986. I was shopping in Soho and saw in a store window a sweater that I wanted to buy for my mother. I pressed my round brown face to the window

5 · THE TEACHER AND VOCATION   157

and my finger to the buzzer, seeking admittance. A narrow-eyed, white teenager wearing running shoes and feasting on bubble gum glared out, evaluating me for signs that would pit me against the limits of his social understanding. After about five seconds, he mouthed "We're closed," and blew pink rubber at me. It was two Saturdays before Christmas, at one o'clock in the afternoon; there were several white people in the store who appeared to be shopping for things for *their* mothers.

I was enraged. At that moment I literally wanted to break all the windows of the store and *take* lots of sweaters for my mother. In the flicker of his judgmental gray eyes, that saleschild had transformed my brightly sentimental, joy-to-the-world, pre-Christmas spree to a shambles. He snuffed my sense of humanitarian catholicity, and there was nothing I could do to snuff his, without making a spectacle of myself.

I am still struck by the structure of power that drove me into such a blizzard of rage. There was almost nothing I could do, short of physically intruding upon him, that would humiliate him the way he humiliated me. No words, no gestures, no prejudices of my own would make a bit of difference to him; his refusal to let me into the store—it was Benetton's, whose colorfully punnish ad campaign is premised on wrapping every one of the world's peoples in its cottons and woolens—was an outward manifestation of his never having let someone like me into the realm of his reality. He had no compassion, no remorse, no reference to me; and no desire to acknowledge me even at the estranged level of arm's-length transactor. He saw me only as one who would take his money and therefore could not conceive that I was there to give him money. In this weird ontological imbalance, I realized that buying something in that store was like bestowing a gift, the gift of my commerce, the lucre of my patronage. In the wake of my outrage, I wanted to take back the gift of appreciation that my peering in the window must have appeared to be. I wanted to take it back in the form of unappreciation, disrespect, defilement. I wanted to work so hard at wishing he could feel what I felt that he would never again mistake my hatred for some sort of plaintive wish to be included. I was quite willing to disenfranchise myself, in the heat of my need to revoke the flattery of my purchasing power. I was willing to boycott Benetton's, random white-owned businesses, and anyone who ever blew bubble gum in my face again.

My rage was admittedly diffuse, even self-destructive, but it was symmetrical. The perhaps loose-ended but utter propriety of that rage is no doubt lost not just to the young man who actually barred me, but to those who would appreciate my being barred only as an abstract precaution, who approve of those who would bar even as they deny that they would bar *me*.

The violence of my desire to burst into Benetton's is probably quite apparent. I often wonder if the violence, the exclusionary hatred, is equally apparent in the repeated public urgings that blacks understand the buzzer system by putting themselves in the shoes of white store owners—that, in effect, blacks look into the mirror of frightened white faces for the reality of their undesirability; and that then blacks would "just as surely conclude that [they] would not let [themselves] in under similar circumstances." (That some blacks might agree merely shows that some of us have learned too well the lessons of privatized intimacies of self-hatred and rationalized away the fullness of our public, participatory selves.)

On the same day I was barred from Benetton's, I went home and wrote the above impassioned account in my journal. On the day after that, I found I was still brooding, so I turned to a form of catharsis I have always found healing. I typed up as much of the story as I have just told, made a big poster of it, put a nice colorful border around it, and, after Benetton's was truly closed, stuck it to their big sweater-filled window. I exercised my first-amendment right to place my business with them right out in

5 · THE TEACHER AND VOCATION

the Street. So that was the first telling of this story. The second telling came a few months later, for a symposium on Excluded Voices sponsored by a law review. I wrote an essay summing up my feelings about being excluded from Benetton's and analyzing "how the rhetoric of increased privatization, in response to racial issues, functions as the rationalizing agent of public unaccountability and, ultimately, irresponsibility." Weeks later, I received the first edit. From the first page to the last, my fury had been carefully cut out. My rushing, run-on-rage had been reduced to simple declarative sentences. The active personal had been inverted in favor of the passive impersonal. My words were different; they spoke to me upside down. I was afraid to read too much of it at a time—meanings rose up at me oddly, stolen and strange.

A week and a half later, I received the second edit. All reference to Benetton's had been deleted because, according to the editors and the faculty adviser, it was defamatory; they feared harassment and liability; they said printing it would be irresponsible. I called them and offered to supply a footnote attesting to this as my personal experience at one particular location and of a buzzer system not limited to Benetton's; the editors told me that they were not in the habit of publishing things that were unverifiable. I could not but wonder, in this refusal even to let me file an affidavit, what it would take to make my experience verifiable. The testimony of an independent white bystander? (a requirement in fact imposed in U.S. Supreme Court holdings through the first part of the century).

Two days *after* the piece was sent to press, I received copies of the final page proofs. All reference to my race had been eliminated because it was against "editorial policy" to permit descriptions of physiognomy. "I realize," wrote one editor, "that this was a very personal experience, but any reader will know what you must have looked like when standing at that window." In a telephone conversation to them, I ranted wildly about the significance of such an omission. "It's irrelevant," another editor explained in a voice gummy with soothing and patience; "It's nice and poetic," but it doesn't "advance the discussion of any principle ... This is a law review, after all." Frustrated, I accused him of censorship; calmly he assured me it was not. "This is just a matter of style," he said with firmness and finality.

Ultimately I did convince the editors that mention of my race was central to the whole sense of the subsequent text; that my story became one of extreme paranoia without the information that I am black; or that it became one in which the reader had to fill in the gap by assumption, presumption, prejudgment, or prejudice. What was most interesting to me in this experience was how the blind application of principles of neutrality, through the device of omission, acted either to make me look crazy or to make the reader participate in old habits of cultural bias....

Spend some time with your journal exploring your responses to this excerpt. If you're working with a colleague or colleagues, share and discuss your responses; explore how you differ.

Can you imagine yourself writing this way, or do you agree with the editors or have another perspective? How does your personal experience figure into your writing.

One teacher can identify.

... I've been thinking about the role of "feeling" in "thinking"-dominated legal scholarship. Lately I've been reading books by Mary-Louise von Franz, a Jungian analyst who specialized in the interpretation of fairy tales. She cautioned that "thinking" types are prone to over-analyze the structure of fairy tales and completely miss the "feeling" of the story. It reminded me of the Patricia Williams story about the NY Benetton store. Were the law review editors uncomfortable with her emotional story because it was her personal story, or were they uncomfortable because her story was so full of feeling, which thinking types

5 · THE TEACHER AND VOCATION

don't "get" or value? Recall that I told the Sleeping Lady group that I included poetry in my law review article on the tax consequences of fertility treatment … [T]he poetry conveys strong feeling in a manner that is unusual in law review articles. I was free to write my fertility cost article in any way I wanted, because I had been tenured, so I included the poetry without regard for the way in which it would be received by student editors of law reviews. Ironically, the article was accepted by the Cornell Law Review![26]

Can you imagine encouraging your students to write this way?* You've seen some examples of this form of student writing in Chapter 3.

Thinking about your own writing, does it have a distinctive voice, and if so, how would you describe that voice? Can you describe the voice you'd like to have as a writer, or in academic writing, do you think that as an author, you should recede or withdraw as much as possible? Mary Rose O'Reilley argues that voiceless writing is inert, unpersuasive.

But finding voice—let's be clear—is a political act. It defines a moment of presence, of being awake; and it involves not only self-understanding, but the ability to transmit that self-understanding to others. Learning to write so that you will be read, therefore, vitalizes both the

---

* Here's Mary Rose O'Reilley on this question:
 … We do not try to teach students a civil tongue (to which I would have no objection) but rather some hideous in-group jargon. Too many of us teachers speak (and therefore pass on) the gabble of sociology or education, one of the new Derridean dialects, or a lumpy feminism. Depending on their intelligence, musical ear, or level of desperation, students do or do not learn to sound like us. The more crafty among them will argue, parroting a professorial opinion, that technical vocabulary is essential to every trade. Because I teach a lot of theology students, I like to tell them that if Jesus had talked like that, he would never have made it out of Nazareth.
O'Reilley, *Peaceable Classroom*, 55–56.

162   5 · THE TEACHER AND VOCATION

self and the community. Voiceless writing, as Peter Elbow has observed, drains the reader; writing that has a voice in it gives energy … Perhaps scientists will some day discover that it quickens our heartbeat and warms the extremities. By contrast, as Elbow has also noted, to experience yourself as "voiceless" is a definition of depression, subjugation, and being counted out … To "have a voice" is to have authority.

The other day as I was reading the first chapter of Mark's gospel, I came upon the familiar passage where Jesus begins his career of teaching and driving out demons. "He has authority," the people say. "He doesn't talk like the Scribes."

The next question I had to ask was, "How did the Scribes talk?"

Well, I suppose nowadays we would call it "academic discourse."[27]

Do you agree with O'Reilley and Elbow and consequently, think Patricia Williams's essay has authority? Parker Palmer would.

… Authority is granted to people who are perceived as *authoring* their own words, their own actions, their own lives, rather than playing a scripted role at great remove from their own hearts.[28]

However, when in a graduate course Mark asked a group of LL.M students to read Williams' piece, most of them found it totally inappropriate. They felt she was angry, felt a journal article was no place for anger. The piece was too personal. Perhaps you agree? Do the contrary voices in Williams' piece make more sense to you?

Do these students' strongly negative responses reflect the culture in which they live, in which " 'Don't wear your heart on your sleeve' and 'Hold your cards close to your vest' are … two examples of (the lesson taught) from an early age that 'masked and divided' is the safe and sane way to live?"[29]

Will living by those precepts sustain a life lived in vocation? That's the question that frames Kazuo Ishiguro's beautifully realized novel, *The Remains of the Day*.[30] It tells the story of

5 · THE TEACHER AND VOCATION 163

Stevens, an English butler, whose life is a sustained attempt to live by those lessons.* Through a long career serving an English gentleman, Stevens works hard to maintain his conception of professionalism, which for him means rigidly separating his personal feelings from his professional behavior. Adhering to that conception means ignoring his personal objections and following his master's orders to fire two Jewish maids in the middle of the Second World War. It means remaining at his post throughout an important conference when he knows his father is in a room upstairs dying. It means refusing to express his love for a co-worker, who, frustrated by Stevens's rigidity, leaves to marry a man she doesn't love. It even may mean losing his soul. These are heavy losses, and reviewing and attempting to justify his life, Stevens is full of regret.

Are these the inevitable consequences of living a divided life? Parker Palmer thinks so; he suggests that "disappear(ing) into our roles," as Stevens did, is extremely costly. Among these costs, all of which Stevens experiences:

- We sense that something is missing in our lives and search the world for it, not understanding that what is missing is us.
- We feel fraudulent, even invisible, because we are not in the world as we really are.
- Our inauthenticity and projections make real relationships impossible, leading to loneliness. [Stevens often projects orders or responses onto his master, never checking to determine whether his projections are correct. Throughout the novel he remains alone.]
- Our contributions to the world—especially through the work we do—are tainted by duplicity and deprived of the life-giving energies of the true self.[31]

---

* On the persuasive power of stories, novelist Tobias Wolff reminds us through one of his central characters that "[t]he truth of ... stories didn't come as a set of theories. You [feel] it in the back of your neck."
Tobias Wolff, *Old School* (New York: Knopf 2003), 97.

164   5 · THE TEACHER AND VOCATION

We agree with Ishiguro and Palmer, and in writing this book, have tried to reflect on a similar message about the virtues of living an integrated life. Do *you* agree? If so, spend some time thinking how what you write expresses yourself and what you might do to enhance that expression. You might identify writing that engages you, try to identify what about it is engaging, and then reflect on whether any of those strategies would work for you. If you don't agree, explore what about your writing sustains you in your vocation.

B. Classroom Teaching

Teachers teach who they are.*

Consider the following story.

… I had an interesting experience in my Contracts class in August … It was the first week of school. I teach Contracts three days a week, including Friday. My best friend had been very ill with cancer for three years. She died on the Thursday night of the first week of school. I was at her house most of the night, and I cried for most of the night, but I decided to teach my class on Friday, in part because I felt like doing something positive, and in part because I thought that I (might) have to miss a class the next week for the funeral. I had puffy red eyes and looked a bit strange, so I decided that I needed to tell the students what had happened.

It didn't go quite as planned! I said what had happened in a sentence or two; when I said that my best friend had died the night before, I burst into tears (the unplanned part). It took me a minute or two to compose myself, after which the rest of the class proceeded in the normal fashion. The students were very kind to me after the class.

---

* Multiple Sources. Compare Parker Palmer:
   *Good teaching cannot be reduced to technique: good teaching comes
   from the identity and integrity of the teacher.*
Palmer, *Courage to Teach*, 10.

5 · THE TEACHER AND VOCATION

One told me how much he respected the fact that I came to teach them; another student offered me a hug ("No, not a little hug" she said. "You need a BIG hug.").

I felt that it was a mark of my growth as a teacher that I didn't feel embarrassed for being who I was at that time. I just appreciated their kindness. The students got together after class and bought me several condolence cards. The entire section signed the cards. I was very touched.

That was all very interesting, but the most interesting thing is the effect that this interaction had on our classroom dynamic. There is a different, and better, dynamic in this class than in my typical first-year class, and I suspect that it is because they fear me less than my students usually do. I never intend for my students to fear me, but they often do fear me; they tell me later that my intensity and knowledge intimidated them. By accidentally showing some vulnerability in front of them early in the term, I came off as a fellow human being, not just a scary law professor. And I saw my students as compassionate human beings in return. The mood in the class is very friendly and supportive. Next year, my challenge will be to try to get to the same place intentionally.[32]

It can be as important to be present in your teaching as it is in your writing.* What does or would being present in your teaching

---

* Gonzaga Law Professor and Director of the Institute of Law School Teaching Gerry Hess puts it this way:

Teacher Presence

One type of communication linked to effective teaching is teacher immediacy. Immediacy refers to verbal and non-verbal communication that brings teacher and student closer together. A teacher's immediacy behaviors reflect a positive attitude toward students and enhance personal relationships with students; they potentially influence students' attitudes toward the teacher and the course and improve student learning. An empirical study of college students revealed the types of teacher immediacy behavior that enhanced learning for white, Hispanic, Asian, and Black students. The

166   5 · THE TEACHER AND VOCATION

mean for you? Perhaps you make different choices than this writer did. What choices *do* you make?

Not only do we think it's important to be present to our students; we also think we need to be present to our subjects, to establish meaningful relationships with them. The argument for distance in relation to our subjects parallels the ones made for maintaining distance from our students and "objectivity" in our writing. Parker Palmer asserts that as in academic writing, in education, "objectivism" is the dominant mode of knowing.[33] Palmer suggests that this mode dominates, because we're fearful of "contaminating" what we're seeking to know with our own perspective. That leads us to ask a similar question here to the one we asked about our relationship to students: If a stranger were to visit a classroom in which we embraced a meaningful relationship between knower and known, what would they see? If that picture isn't one you recognize, what can you do to enact it?

IV. Conclusion

What if we had nothing to prove? We end this section as we began, where authentic thinking about vocation must end. The question of vocation, as Fowler suggests, is a lifelong one, for everyday. Finding your way to reflect richly about this question,

---

verbal behaviors that demonstrated engagement and significantly affected learning for all four groups included soliciting alternative viewpoints and opinions from students; praising student work; calling students by name; posing questions end encouraging students to talk; using humor; having discussion outside the class; and asking students how they feel about assignments. Two non-verbal behaviors significantly affected learning for all four ethnic groups: maintaining eye contact and smiling at students.

Another behavior critical to engagement is listening. Teachers communicate their presence to students by listening carefully to student responses and questions. Actual listening takes effort ...
Gerald Hess, "Heads and Hearts: The Teaching and Learning Environment in Law School," *Journal of Legal Education* 10 (2002): 101–102.

daily and longitudinally, will also enrich and enliven your teaching life. We would be delighted to hear about other ideas for supporting this important ongoing inquiry for a reflective teacher.

Notes

1. Wayne C. Booth, *The Vocation of a Teacher: Rhetorical Occasions* (Chicago: The University of Chicago Press, 1988), 219.

2. Parker J. Palmer, *The Courage to Teach: Exploring the Inner Landscape of a Teacher's Life* (San Francisco: Jossey-Bass, 1998), 30.

3. Booth, *Rhetorical Occasions*, 251. And later:

To love students in the sense of wanting to teach them is a virtue; to want to be loved and admired is usually a mistake and often a vice ... When the desire to be loved takes over, it can lead the teacher, as it leads political candidates, into grotesque oscillations from displays of benevolence to excessive gestures designed to prove toughness.

Ibid., at 253.

4. Jane Tompkins, *A Life in School: What the Teacher Learned* (Reading, MA: Addison Wesley, 1996).

5. Frederick Buechner, *Wishful Thinking: The Seeker's ABCs* (New York: HarperOne, 1993), 119.

6. Palmer, *Courage to Teach*, 148.

7. Ibid., 148.

8. Ibid., 148–49.

9. Mary Rose O'Reilley, *Radical Presence: Teaching as a Contemplative Practice* (Portsmouth, NH: Boynton/Cook, 1998), 40–41.

10. Ibid., 41.

11. Ibid., 41.

12. Mark Weisberg, "Epilogue: When (Law) Students Write," *Legal Studies Forum* 27 (2003): 421–36.

13. Karen W. Saakvitne and Laurie Anne Pearlman, *Transforming the Pain: Workbook on Vicarious Traumatization* (New York: W. W. Norton & Company Inc., 1996).

14. James W. Fowler, *Becoming Adult, Becoming Christian: Adult Development & Christian Faith* (San Francisco: Jossey-Bass, 2000), 83–85.

15. Mary Rose O'Reilley, *The Peaceable Classroom* (Portsmouth, NH: Boynton/Cook, 1993), 90–91. For an exploration of what it might mean in a course to shift from discerning the gifted to discerning the gift, see Mark Weisberg, "Discerning the Gift," *Change: The Magazine of Higher Learning* 31, no. 3 (1999): 28–37.

16. Fowler, *Becoming Adult, Becoming Christian*, quoted at 130 above, in "From Career to Vocation," #4.

17. Donald L. Finkel and G. Stephen Monk, "Dissolution of the Atlas Complex," in *Learning in Groups: New Directions for Teaching and Learning*, no. 14, eds. Clark Bouton and Russell Y. Garth (San Francisco: Jossey-Bass, 1983).

18. O'Reilley, *Peaceable Classroom*, 84.

19. Tompkins, *A Life in School*, 48.

5 · THE TEACHER AND VOCATION   169

20. Annie Dillard, *The Writing Life* (New York: Harper & Row, 1989), 23.

21. Doris Kearns Goodwin narrates the tale of the conception of lend-lease and its implementation in, *No Ordinary Time: Franklin and Eleanor Roosevelt: The Home Front In World War II* (New York: Touchstone, 1994), 190–96, 201–202, and 210–15. Roosevelt and his wife Eleanor had an almost diametrically opposed set of internal and external processes they could trust, also detailed in the history. For another fascinating account of two radically differing working styles, see Ann Patchett, *Truth and Beauty* (New York: Harper Collins, 2004).

22. For a full account of what changing entailed, see Weisberg, "Discerning the Gift."

23. Scott Sellers, "Discovering What Matters: An Interview with Wayson Choy," *READ Magazine*, Vol. 5, Issue 1 (2004), 35–39.

24. A quote attributed to E.B. White in the profile by Israel Shenker, "E.B. White: Notes and Comment by Author" *The New York Times*, August 3, 1997, last accessed January 21, 2011, http://www.nytimes.com/books/97/08/03/lifetimes/white-notes.html.

25. Reprinted by permission of the publisher from "The Death of the Profane" in Patricia J. Williams, *The Alchemy of Race and Rights: Diary of a Law Professor* (Cambridge: Harvard University Press, Copyright © 1991 by the President and Fellows of Harvard College), 44–48.

26. Katherine Pratt, Law Professor, reflecting on being present in what she writes in an e-mail to Mark Weisberg, November 18, 2004.

27. O'Reilley, *Radical Presence*, 58.

28. Palmer, *Courage to Teach*, 33.

29. Parker J. Palmer, *A Hidden Wholeness: The Journey Toward an Undivided Life* (San Francisco: Jossey-Bass, 2004), 15–16.

30. Kazuo Ishiguro, *The Remains of Day* (New York: Knopf, 1989).

31. Palmer, *Hidden Wholeness*, 15–16.

32. Katherine Pratt reflecting following the 2003 *Reflecting on Our Teaching* retreat, held in Leavenworth, Washington, in an e-mail to Mark Weisberg, October 1, 2003.

33. Palmer, *Courage to Teach*, 51–52.

Chapter 6

How Does a Teacher Say Goodbye?

Don't cry because it's over. Smile because it happened …
—Proverb

How lucky I am to have something that makes saying good-
bye so hard.
—Anonymous

I. Introduction

Exercise: Think about the semester most recently past.

a) *How did you say goodbye to your class, and your stu-*
    dents?
b) *How did it go? Would you change anything about it in*
    the future?

During a teaching life, even during a single course, teachers
say many goodbyes, and those goodbyes rarely are easy. At first,
this may seem odd. The work of the semester is ending or over;
transitions to new classes or through graduation are long rou-
tinized. Indeed, many teachers may well not focus on goodbye,
or prioritize it. Why do we, and why do we claim goodbyes are
difficult?

Like most teachers, we have crawled to the end of more than
a few semesters, just eking through the last class or grading the
last exam. We know the fatigue, the relinquished aspirations, the
depleted energy that often accompanies the end of a semester,
just at a time when new energies are needed: to grade, to sum

up, to review, to complete all that was promised, to turn around and get ready for the next semester, year, class. Time marches from one "to do" item to another, as all our obligations come to roost. In the midst of all of that activity, why is goodbye important?

It's important, because during the occasions when we've stopped to reflect and mark an ending or transition, we, and, we believe, our students, have been deeply enriched. Often, when we've paused and picked up our heads from our grinding "to do" list, we've experienced something remarkable, even beautiful—the spread of the semester behind us, the long journey travelled, the deep thinking, hard work, and meetings of minds that have comprised what we and our students have learned and how we've grown. For teachers yearning for reflection, ending times are rich in insight and unique in opportunity; that also can be true for our students. Goodbyes offer us one final way to embody our teaching goals and to perform the messages of the course. Teachers have a unique opportunity to point out and enrich goodbyes in service of their students' learning, pausing in the flow of time to appreciate, review, and integrate.

Of course, we must be gentle with ourselves about lost opportunities at goodbye. Sometimes we are too overwhelmed or too busy, and we must respect that goodbyes cannot be forced. But our positive experiences with goodbyes convince us that a thoughtful, reflective goodbye can cap a teaching and learning experience and deepen it. In addition, planning from the start for a learning experience to include such a goodbye, and planting seeds during the course, allows goodbye to become an integral part of an entire learning experience rather than an isolated moment. It also helps emphasize what we have learned over time—that the cycle of teaching and learning can be enriched by the unique attention and possibilities offered only at the end.

Every teacher-student and teacher-class relationship ends, or changes into a new relationship entirely. Our semester is bounded by these planned, foreseen ends: final exams, graduation, end of semester gatherings. Still, like other professionals who have acknowledged the end of a relationship, we more thoroughly and more comfortably focus on hellos to the exclusion of goodbyes. This appears to be a natural human tendency, rooted in a discomfort our society has with ending relationships and facing loss. Some commentators have suggested that our failure on a professional level to discuss endings reflects a tendency towards denial that pervades the entire process of ending a professional relationship.[1] Mental health and social work professionals now regularly study and acknowledge what they call the "termination phase" of the professional relationship.

Unlike therapists and patients, teachers and students are not used to calling an official end to a relationship. To be sure, some teachers and students will remain in touch over the succeeding years. But teachers will never again reconvene a particular class of students; most teachers lose touch with most students after they leave; and those relationships that do continue do so in a new frame: recommender, colleague, friend. Both student and teacher deeply need closure to finish a fruitful partnership in learning, at the time that it naturally ends. After carefully attempting to teach students respectfully and thoughtfully, a teacher might contradict those messages by leaving the student's world without saying goodbye. A teacher who says farewell in a way that underscores and reflects the central values of the learning experience, seals and exponentially multiplies those messages in a bounded, coherent whole. A teacher who ignores the goodbye process can diminish the gains accomplished in the class or teacher-student relationship, and can discourage students in their later education.

Unfortunately, the reality that goodbyes occur regularly in a teacher's life doesn't make them any easier. And because students have so much less experience with saying goodbye, facilitating goodbyes can be challenging for teachers. Unlike our students, who only go through school once, we can see goodbyes coming, have time to plan for them, and have more experience with their challenges. Being better placed to point out an ending and make the best use of it, we need to attend to its design.

Since we think goodbyes are such a significant element in educational experiences, and since they come at the end of those ex-

174   6 · HOW DOES A TEACHER SAY GOODBYE?

periences, we've chosen to close this book with our reflections on these critical, difficult, and wistful staples of a teaching life.

II. Invitations for Thinking about Goodbye

Here are ten prompts. Take a moment and jot down your responses to them. Try for detail: when was it; where were you; who was your interlocutor; what were your feelings; what do you feel/think now?

1. What did you do to end your last class?
2. What was the most fulfilling goodbye you ever said? The least?
3. Can you remember a time when you wanted to say goodbye but didn't?
4. Can you remember an important goodbye a teacher said to you? A note in your Yearbook? A final handshake at graduation?
5. Can you remember a time when a student said goodbye to you? Jean remembers one.

Jean had worked closely with Matt, a student who first represented asylum clients under her supervision and then worked as her research assistant on a chapter in her book on representing children about ending the lawyer-child client relationship. They discussed, daily, the complications of saying goodbye in the professional relationship, the unexpected complexity of the process, the propensity to deny the necessity of termination, and creative solutions to breaking through that denial. As graduation approached, Matt got a job in town and prepared to study for the bar.

At Matt's graduation, Jean, full of pride and emotion, warmly greeted Matt and his parents. As she hugged Matt, she said, "Thank heavens, this isn't the end—since you're staying in town." Matt stopped short, looked her straight in the eye, and said, "NO! We know better. We must say good-

bye now, because our relationship is fundamentally changing. Please say goodbye to me! When we get together later, we'll start our new relationship."

6. Can you remember a time when a goodbye made an important difference in a relationship?

7. Have you been at a session in which you were intrigued by a goodbye someone said or an exercise someone facilitated?

8. Complete the following sentence twelve times: When I think about goodbye, I feel _____.

9. Do you have a favorite goodbye from a book? A movie? The theatre?

10. I don't understand why goodbye merits so much attention. Do you agree?

Consider the following story, told by one of Jean's research assistants.

In one course, her teacher had walked into class the first day and just started into the substance of the law—no prologue, no introductions, no broad context. It was as if he was continuing a conversation that the students would join immediately. On the last day of class, the teacher spoke about substance until the last moment of the lecture, finished a sentence, and walked out.

Even when we don't plan for and don't explicitly say goodbye to our students, we're still always saying goodbye. We offer end of term reviews; we examine our students; we grade them; we may provide feedback on their papers or review their exams. Even walking out of class at the end of term without saying a word is a goodbye. This particular goodbye actually did send a consistent message with its companion hello; it performed the message of an ongoing discourse in the field that the students had entered, and then left. Like our curriculum, each of these activities sends a message, tells our students what we care about.

176   6 · HOW DOES A TEACHER SAY GOODBYE?

Remember our concern about entrainment, at the beginning of a semester? Were you successful in achieving a collaborative rhythm with your students? Now, as they leave, to start other classes, to graduate, while you maintain the steady academic life, goodbye requires letting go of walking in step with your students. What particular challenges will that pose for you?

Think about your end of term activities and reflect on the messages they may send to your students. Are they the messages you want to send? The ones you want to say goodbye with?

III. Ideas for Last Classes/Meetings

Here are several ideas we've used in final classes, usually small seminars.

A. A Closing Circle

A closing circle offers everyone a space in which to say a parting thought. Often this is best done without notice, so people don't feel required to write a speech or be thorough in their thoughts. We prefer spontaneous statements in the moment. Here are several possible structures for the closing circle:

- Start in a circle. The first person goes and every person can pass or say something. At the end quickly ask if the people who passed want to add anything.
- Variation. Ask anyone to start and then ask anyone to go next as they feel moved. In all the variations, the first person often sets a tone.
- Variation. Ask for moment of beauty from the semester
- Variation. Ask: "What have you learned this semester, or what are you taking away?"

B. Completing the Circle

You might link hello and goodbye by repeating an exercise with which you began the course. For example, you might open the

6 · HOW DOES A TEACHER SAY GOODBYE?   177

course asking students to write down their goals for the course and to save them. During the last class you can ask them to look at those goals and reflect on whether they've been met, or revised, and to reflect on what that might mean for them.

At the retreat described in the Preface and Chapter 1, we had asked the participants to take a piece of ribbon or yarn and tie a knot in it for each issue they hoped to reflect upon during the retreat. During the second half of the retreat, we invited them back to the art table and asked them to use the ribbon or yarn make a talisman to memorialize the lessons of the retreat.

One participant wrote us later, "I think of that retreat daily, honestly, as I have, hanging on my fridge, the 'talisman' … that many of us made on our half-day 'off.' The words still ring true to me daily, 'Let go, move on, stay home, slow down, reflect'—I've done all 5 of these things since that retreat, and I'm better for it."

As reported in Chapter 1, Mark often begins a course, asking students to write down what they're looking forward to in a life in the law, what they're fearful of, and what they're looking forward to and fearful of in the course. Students write their responses, then share them with a small group, after which Mark invites comments. Similarly to the goals exercise, on the last day, you might repeat all or part of this one.

By the way, did you write down answers to the opening questions of this book when you looked at our first chapter? If so, take a look at those reflections and thoughts now. They may offer ideas for ending this phase of your reflection process, or for starting a new cycle of reflection.

C. Jean's Goodbye and Coupon

As a clinical law teacher, Jean works closely with her students in their first semester, talking and emailing multiple times daily, deeply planning, debriefing and reflecting on intense emotional topics concerning her child clients' anguish at being separated from their families, or her asylum client's struggle to recount the maltreatment and fear that caused her to leave her home country. Early in her career, she discovered that the transition from the end

178   6 · HOW DOES A TEACHER SAY GOODBYE?

of an intense semester together to a semester of little or no contact, or the transition that comes when a student is graduating, was invariably awkward and difficult for her. On the one hand, the work had ended, new students awaited her, and it was time to end this relationship and begin others. Jean is an irregular correspondent and, as a full-time professor with small children at home, she knew that she would only disappoint students who expected their relationship to continue at the same level of intensity and consistency. On the other hand, her intense experience with each student gave her both substantial insight into the student's strengths, weaknesses, likes and dislikes as professionals, and a deep investment in their prosperity and happiness after law school. How to say a proper goodbye?

Jean decided to offer an unusual solution that involved making a promise she knew she could keep. As the end of the working relationship approached, she talked about her limited availability in the future, and committed to be available for references and letters of recommendation, but warned that other tasks would be harder to complete. However, she did offer each student a "coupon" for future use. "At some point in the future, maybe 5 days, 5 weeks, 5 months, or 5 years, you may encounter a moment when you think that input from me would make a substantial useful difference. At that point, email or call me, and let me know that you are cashing your coupon. On that date, you move to the top of my priority list, along with my current students, current clients, and family, and I will get back to you immediately."

D. Postcards and Silent Witness

In *A Life in School,* Jane Tompkins composes a series of postcards, the kind you write but do not send. You've already seen several; here are two more examples:

Dear Students,

When I pay attention to the subject matter in class, instead of to you, I get excited, think of an idea that just *has* to be said, blurt it out, and, more often than not, kill something. As in the Dickinson poem: "My life had stood/A loaded gun/In corners ..."

When I speak the report is so loud it deafens. No one can hear anything but what I said. Discussion dies. It seems it's either you or me, my authority or your power to speak. What do I do that shuts people up? Or is this a false dilemma? Help!

Sincerely,
Jane

_____

Dear Colleagues:

Here's a joke I remember from junior high school, or maybe it was college. A woman went to the doctor and said, "Doctor, I have this enormous desire to eat pancakes. I just can't get enough of them. What can I do?" "Well," said the doctor, "that doesn't sound too serious. How many pancakes are we talking about?" "Oh," said the woman, "at home I have sixteen chests full."

When it comes to knowledge, we are like that woman. At home we have sixteen chests full, and we're dying to get our hands on sixteen more. But since even one cold pancake is too many, why are we doing this?

Jane[2]

In his last classes, Mark often distributes a group of these postcards, which have been mounted on cardboard to look like postcards, each with a number indicating the sequence in which they appear. He asks each student with a card to read his aloud, and we proceed through the sequence. Mark then invites students to write their own postcards, and if they're willing, to place them on a board or a wall, ideally around the room.

Class ends with a "silent witness," during which class members move quietly and read the postcards, without comment. Often the postcards are moving, offering glimpses into each person's experience of their education or of an important relationship, celebrated or mourned. A collective moment of reflection.

IV. Goodbye:
A Unique Moment of Reflection

The above exercises suggest that it's in the moment of ending that we fully feel the losses and gifts of an experience. However, some goodbyes are much longer than these. Mark is on a sabbatical, following which he'll retire. Anticipating this time, he's gradually been reducing his university commitments. In what follows, he reflects on his impending retirement.

A Long Goodbye

Five words: Relief, Concern, Gratitude, Fulfillment, Disappointment. Conflicting emotions, each of which I have felt during the past several months, separately, and occasionally, simultaneously.

I feel them now, sitting in my almost empty office, soon to leave it forever. I'm retiring. Almost retiring. First a sabbatical, an officeless sabbatical;[3] then retirement. This follows several years teaching all courses in one term, in turn followed by reducing my commitment to ¾ time, and now, a half sabbatical. Downsizing gradually: a long goodbye. One for which I've tried to prepare.

I've always felt it important at the end of a course, to offer an opportunity for my students and myself to achieve closure. Even at the end of a class. For example, borrowing an idea from my friend Don Finkel,[4] in Legal Imagination, which is a writing course, I set aside the last 15 minutes of each class for students to record in a (private) journal their thoughts and responses to that day's readings and class discussion. Several moments of silent reflection.

At the end of a course, I've used activities we describe in this book: letter to self, postcards and silent witness, facilitating a closing circle, with each person saying to their peers and to me whatever they'd like to say.

But a year of goodbye—how to do that? Start with Hello, I thought. Mark this year as special. An idea presented itself immediately. In the previous winter, in a course on persuasion, I had traded on Jean's "Thing of Beauty." For the first five minutes of each class, a student would bring to class something that to them was beautiful, present it, and explain why they found it beautiful. I transposed that

6 · HOW DOES A TEACHER SAY GOODBYE?   181

to Five Minutes of Persuasion. The students quickly embraced the idea, and we experienced paintings, photographic essays, songs, and in one case, an original, beautiful musical composition, performed on flute, accompanied by a piano recording, also played by this student.

Sarah's composition and performance were deeply moving, and when the course ended, I asked her if she'd be willing to perform it as the students walked into the first class of my final teaching year. She agreed, and that moving, special hello marked the beginning of a special final year.

We followed that celebratory moment each week with Jean's "Thing of Beauty." The sense of ritual and celebration established in those first five minutes deepened and enriched what for most students always had been a course with intense personal meaning. As one student put it:

> *The Thing of Beauty allowed our class to speak to each other in a way that you don't usually find in Law School. By choosing something that we thought was beautiful and explaining it to the class, we were encouraged to open our minds and our hearts to one another. We peered into each other's souls and in turn we established trust, honesty, respect and confidence. In short, we built a community. Maybe it didn't change our lives, but it sure was a nice way to start the day.**

---

* From class written responses to my request for feedback on whether Thing of Beauty had affected their learning experience in the course. Here are two other responses.

I enjoy the Thing of Beauty, because I consider it an opportunity to learn more about the personalities and interests of our classmates. Otherwise, there isn't much opportunity to learn about each other's talents and interests in such a way. I find the Thing of Beauty adds extra depth and context to the people in class beyond their comments on a particular school subject and creates more of a bond between us. It reminds me that there are aspects of law school that aren't just about mass-producing lawyers by pumping us full of information and marking us against one another. It humanizes us and generates respect among peers, which is important for the legal profession, but sadly, the current model of entering and getting through law school and landing a job drives us to view each

182   6 · HOW DOES A TEACHER SAY GOODBYE?

Early on in that fall term class and in the two winter term classes, I told everyone that this was my last teaching year and that I hoped we would have fun. That felt liberating, and in each course, I felt more relaxed and carefree, more honest and open, than in any other year. I think those courses were better for it. I certainly was.

Wanting to signal in my last class that the end of the course was the end of forty-one years teaching, I chose a moment of silence, accompanied by a recording of Sarah's music.

I left feeling I had done what I needed to do.

That process has felt good, satisfying. But I don't think I'm finished. Strong emotions persist. Hence the Five Words listed above.

Relief

I no longer have to walk into a classroom. But don't I love teaching? Yes; what I love is being excited by an idea, asking a question

---

other as constant competitors for the same positions. Those who don't bother taking the time to get to know their colleagues as people tend to retain this competitive mentality once they get out into the working world. Therefore, I think the Thing of Beauty is important to our learning and hopefully people will consider the larger context of this exercise after law school.

The 'thing of beauty' fit in well with the theme of the course, especially since one of our first assignments involved finding a beautiful piece of writing. It set a nice tone to the class, and marked the evolution between the first class, when many of us did not know each other, until about half way through the class when it became apparent that people's comfort levels had increased. People seemed unsure as to how to react to the thing of beauty at the beginning, I think because we are not used to this honest, unpretentious tone in a law school class. From a group perspective, I think the thing of beauty contributed to breaking the ice between members of the class. From an individual perspective, I think it was an interesting exercise. I spent a long time thinking about what my particular contribution should be; what I think is beautiful, and what would be well received by the class. I spent more time thinking about how to explain what I think is "beautiful", why I think something in particular is beautiful, than I did actually picking the thing itself, and practicing it. That in itself is something that led me to reflect quite a bit on this exercise, adding another dimension to the thing of beauty.

6 · HOW DOES A TEACHER SAY GOODBYE?   183

that prompts reflection and productive conversation, experiencing my students developing distinctive voices, observing them as they struggle to form a community.

I don't love preparing for classes and find myself less and less looking forward to them. Nor do I enjoy looking at omnipresent laptops rather than full faces, even when we've developed a class protocol for using them.

I don't like feeling stressed as I try to balance my commitments to my teaching and to my family. I notice how much more relaxed I am when I'm away from it.

And sometimes, more often lately, I don't feel I belong. I'm too many generations distant from the current group of students, and although I have a ten-year-old daughter, don't "get" them.

Mostly, though, I'm tired.

Concern

What will I do now? Fritter my time away? I've always relied on the daily routine imposed by teaching to keep me organized, regulated. Sabbaticals have been a nightmare. Even summers can be problematic. And with a lovely computer screen beckoning …

Yes, there's the gym, and there are children and grandchildren to visit, as well as one child at home, but will I be faithful?

I'm losing my office. It's been a refuge—a safe, comforting space. It's my preferred writing space. I have a lovely study at home, but I've yet to establish a writing rhythm there. And my wife is moving her study upstairs, next to mine. She's a writer and will spend her days and evenings there. How will that feel? Will I be able to relax into my space?

Colleagues. They're not my closest friends, but I've enjoyed the frequent brief exchanges. At the office, I'm recognized. What will it mean not to have that?

And of course, there's aging …

Fulfillment

When my ex-wife and I drove into Kingston in July 1969, we looked at each other and said, "One year." Forty-one years later, we're both still here. Happy to be here.

184   6 · HOW DOES A TEACHER SAY GOODBYE?

How fulfilled? I've been able to grow as a teacher. I began teaching as I'd been taught, even more ferociously, half believing that showing people what was wrong with their arguments, pressing them to respond on the spot, produced meaningful learning. Half believing, because I also sensed teaching as I did was more about proving how smart I was than about helping students learn, more about responding to my own insecurity than expressing any deeply felt convictions about learning.

I've changed, become less interested in proving myself, more interested in exploring how I can encourage students to become more confident in their abilities. I've become quieter, more patient, more encouraging, and, I think, a better version of my earlier self. I like myself better, feel more integrated. Growing as a teacher has meant growing as a person.

I've felt recognized, by peers and by students. The surface recognition has come as awards: national, provincial, university-wide. What's mattered more deeply has been what's accompanied those awards: the supporting letters people have written. Learning what their experiences with me have meant to them as persons as well as students or colleagues, hearing that they've experienced me as authentic.

I think I've done as much as I can, improved and developed as much as I'm able.

Disappointment

Only one: No recognition, sometimes even hostility, from my Deans. Despite winning those teaching awards, I'm one of the lower paid faculty members for my age and experience. Were they research awards, I'd be among the highest. I'm disappointed for myself and more important, disappointed that despite claiming to value teaching and research equally, my university doesn't.

Even being recognized for my research has been a struggle. I had to institute a grievance against one Dean's "merit" award to get him, and the University, to acknowledge that the workshops I'd developed as a result of my faculty development and teaching and learning research did constitute research.

Finally, I've been disappointed that since my first Dean stepped down, none of the succeeding Deans has understood their mandate to include walking into my office (or the offices of most of my col-

6 · HOW DOES A TEACHER SAY GOODBYE?

leagues) to ask how I'm doing and ask what they could do to support me. To perform the message they assert, that they're interested in having all colleagues succeed. That's not the institution I had hoped my faculty would be.

Gratitude

To my first Dean, who stuck with me, recommending me for tenure, even though I hadn't written anything.[5] It took me 10 years to find my voice.[6] This was the Dean who did walk into my office, who was interested in me.

To Don Finkel, for more than thirty years of friendship and provocative conversations about teaching and learning; to my wife, Susan Olding, for ongoing support, challenge, writing advice, and listening; and to Jean, for the gift of friendship, and for unending inspiration.

To my students, who, sometimes grudgingly, accepted my invitation to give themselves permission to bring what they cared about to what they were learning. When they did, they produced distinctive, imaginative, insightful work. Their increased confidence was palpable.

I have a sixth word, a phrase actually: **Nothing to Prove.** *As I write, that's how I feel. At least for now.*

V. Conclusion

We've come to the end; how to say goodbye? We've decided to offer two goodbyes, one from each of us. Here goes.

Jean: Reflection never ends! As our teaching continues, the reflection only deepens and widens, to link and mirror new experiences with old, new insights with old, new challenges with old. Dear partners in reflection offer so much wisdom, collective memory, and encouragement. In the end, reflection gives me courage—to question, to try, to risk. Thank you for your openness to these ruminations and invitations. I wish for each of you richness in insight, energy in the daily and gratitude for this life in teaching.

186   6 · HOW DOES A TEACHER SAY GOODBYE?

Mark: As I've mentioned, I often end my courses with a Postcard exercise. At the reflection retreat where I first met Jean, we also ended that way. Although this book isn't a course or a retreat, it has echoes of both. Consequently, it feels appropriate for me to end it with a postcard.

Dear Colleagues,

Learning to trust myself and to speak and write in a voice that feels authentic hasn't been easy, but both have been gifts I cherish. I hope they will prove the same for you. Please remember that while teaching can seem a solitary activity, you are not alone.

Warm wishes,
Mark

Notes

1. For more on termination of relationships in social work and other professions, see Jean's chapter on "Leaving the Child's World," in *Representing Children in Child Protective Proceedings.*

2. Jane Tompkins, *A Life in School: What the Teacher Learned* (Reading, MA: Addison Wesley, 1996), 144, and 149–50.

3. Although I asked to retain my office during my sabbatical, my Dean wanted me out. At first resentful, I now think it's for the best. Let the future be now.

4. Don Finkel, now deceased, was a long-time faculty member at Evergreen State College and the author of *Teaching with Your Mouth Shut* (Portsmouth: Boynton/Cook, 2000).

5. Those were the days. That wouldn't be possible now. Right place, right time.

6. For an account of the precipitating event, see my essay, "Discerning the Gift."

Appendix

Resources for Reflecting

Booth, Wayne. *The Vocation of a Teacher: Rhetorical Occasions.* Chicago: University of Chicago Press, 1988.

Brookfield, Stephen, D. *Becoming a Critically Reflective Teacher.* San Francisco: Jossey-Bass, 1995.

Brookfield, Stephen D., and Preskill, Stephen. *Discussion as a Way of Teaching: Tools and Techniques for Democratic Classrooms.* San Francisco: Jossey-Bass, 1999.

Bryant, Susan. "Collaboration in Law Practice: a Satisfying and Productive Process for a Diverse Profession," in *Vermont Law Review* 17 (1993), 459–531.

Coles, Robert. *The Call of Stories: Teaching and the Moral Imagination.* Boston: Houghton Mifflin, 1989.

Critical Incidents: Video Case Studies of Teaching Problems. Victoria: University of Victoria Centre for Learning and Teaching.

Elbow, Peter. *Embracing Contraries: Explorations in Learning and Teaching.* New York: Oxford University Press, 1986.

Finkel, Donald. *Teaching With Your Mouth Shut.* Portsmouth, NH: Boynton/Cook, 2000.

Goleman, Daniel. *Emotional Intelligence.* New York: Bantam, 1994.

Hess, Gerald F. "Heads and Hearts: The Teaching and Learning Environment in Law School," in *Journal of Legal Education* 52 (2002), 75–111.

Hess, Gerald F. "Learning to Think Like a Teacher: Reflective Journals for Legal Educators," in *Gonzaga Law Review* 38 (2002): 129–54.

Kronman, Anthony. "Legal Ethics and Moral Education," in *Yale Law Journal* 90 (1981), 955–69.

Lakoff, George, and Mark Johnson. *Metaphors We Live By.* Chicago: University of Chicago Press, 1980.

Ogilvy, J. P. "The Use of Journals in Legal Education: a Tool for Reflection," in *Clinical Law Review* 3 (1996), 55–107.

O'Reilley, Mary Rose. *Radical Presence: Teaching as Contemplative Practice.* Portsmouth, NH: Boynton/Cook 1998.

O'Reilley, Mary Rose. *The Peaceable Classroom.* Portsmouth, NH: Boynton/Cook, 1993.

Overall, Christine. "Feeling Fraudulent," Chap. 6, in *A Feminist I: Reflections from Academia.* Peterborough, ON: Broadview Press, 1998.

Palmer, Parker. *The Courage to Teach: Exploring the Inner Landscape of a Teacher's Life.* San Francisco: Jossey-Bass, 1998.

Schon, Donald. "Schools." Chap. 6, in *The Reflective Practitioner: Toward a New Design for Teaching and Learning in the Professions.* San-Francisco: Jossey-Bass, 1987.

Shaffer, Thomas. *Faith and the Professions.* Provo: Brigham Young University Press, 1987.

Syverud, Kent. "Taking Students Seriously: A Guide for New Law Teachers," in *Journal of Legal Education* 43 (1993), 247–59.

Tompkins, Jane. *A Life in School: What the Teacher Learned.* Reading, MA: Addison-Wesley, 1996.

Weisberg, Mark. "Discerning the Gift," in *Change*, May/June 1999, 28–37.

Weisberg, Mark, and Jacalyn Duffin. "Evoking the Moral Imagination," in *Change*, January/February 1995, 20–27.

White, James Boyd. *Heracles' Bow: Essays on the Rhetoric and Poetics of Law.* Madison: University of Wisconsin Press, 1985.

Williams, Patricia. *The Alchemy of Race and Rights.* Cambridge: Harvard University Press, 1991.

About the Authors

Jean Koh Peters is the Sol Goldman Clinical Professor at Yale Law School, where she has taught since 1989. She currently supervises and teaches students representing refugees seeking asylum and children in child protection proceedings. She has frequently presented at the annual Association of American Law Schools (AALS) Clinical Teachers' Conference. She was the recipient of the Yale Law Women Teaching Award in 1999. She is the author of *Representing Children in Child Protection Proceedings: Ethical and Practical Dimensions* (3rd ed., LEXIS Law Publishing, 2007). She also is a mother and wife, quilter, yoga and meditation practitioner, amateur musician, tennis and bridge player, and avid novel reader.

Mark Weisberg taught at the Queen's University Law Faculty for 42 years. He's interested in ethics and professionalism, how people learn and develop as professionals, as well as in all forms of writing. He was cross-appointed to the Faculty of Education, and for 16 years, was Instructional Development Faculty Associate at the Queen's Centre for Teaching and Learning, where he worked with faculty members to improve teaching and learning across the campus. Recently he co-taught a graduate course on teaching and learning for doctoral students interested in a teaching career, and he developed a similar course designed specifically for graduate law students. He's written extensively on teaching and learning and has offered scores of faculty development workshops across North America. For his work with students and teachers he has received provincial, national, and university-wide teaching awards. He lives in Kingston, Ontario, with his wife and eleven-year-old daughter, who is younger than one of her nieces.

Index

A Family's Criminal Legacy, 131
A Feminist I: Reflections from Academia, 131, 190
A Hidden Wholeness, 169
A Jury of Her Peers, 14, 24
A Life in School: What the Teacher Learned, 24, 131, 168, 187, 190
A Tale of Two Cities, 17
Administrative duties, 155
Advocacy for Children and Youth (seminar), 10
Al-Din Rumi, Jalal, 60
Announcements, 9–11, 19
Anxiety, 32, 49, 145
Asylum law, 150
Atlas Complex, 122, 131, 168
Auchincloss, Louis, 80, 92, 131
Authentic, xiv, 14, 27, 29, 30, 46, 129, 166, 184, 186
Authentic selves, xiv, 46, 184
Authority, 113, 162, 179
Awards, faculty, 184
Balance (in life), 65, 69
Banff, Alberta, 8, 41, 50, 52

Beck, Martha N., 109
Becoming a Critically Reflective Teacher, 24, 92, 189
Becoming Adult, Becoming Christian: Adult Development & Christian Faith, 168
Bergman, Paul, 93
Binder, David A., 93
Booth, Wayne, 116, 131, 133–135, 168, 189
Brookfield, Stephen D., xxii, 16, 21, 24, 92, 189
Bryant, Susan, 33, 60, 93, 189
Buechner, Frederick, 4, 133, 135, 168
Call (vocation), 136, 142
Calvin and Hobbes, 24
Cameron, Julia, 60
Canadian Law Teachers' Clinic, 151
Carter, Stephen L., 92, 112, 131
Choy, Wayson, 151, 169
Churchill, Winston, 148
Closing circle, 176, 180
Closure, 173, 180
Coincidence, 150

Coming to Our Senses: Healing Ourselves and the World Through Mindfulness, 60
Communication for the Classroom Teacher, 92
Community (in classroom), 141
Community Service Leaders and Educators Engaged in Service Learning, 60
Compose your obituary (exercise), 138
Concern, 13, 105, 121, 134, 176, 180, 183
Cooper, Pamela J., 92
Coupon (goodbye), 177, 178
Critical Incidents: Video Case Studies of Teaching Problems, 131, 189
Daily processes, 29, 147, 150
Deep gladness, 4, 50, 51, 133, 135, 136, 138, 147
Delight, 8, 60
Democratic classroom, 16
Dickens, Charles, 17
Dillard, Annie, 169
Disappointment, 180, 184
Discerning the Gift (essay), 187
Discovering What Matters: An Interview with Wayson Choy, 169
Discussion as a Way of Teaching, 21, 24, 189
Dispositions, classroom, 7, 15, 16
Divided life, 163
Doubting and believing game, 71, 76

Doubting and believing spectrum, 70, 72, 77–79, 89
Doubting and believing spectrum, Peter Elbow, 70
E.B. White: Notes and Comment by Author, 169
Elbow, Peter, 24, 70, 81, 85, 92, 162, 189
Embracing Contraries, 77, 81, 86, 92, 189
Entering into a contained time or space, xvi
Entrainment, 17, 176
Equitable Awards, 80, 92, 131
Eulogy (writing exercise), 138, 140
Expecting Adam, 131
External processes, 89, 148, 153, 169
Fancy, Alex, 47
Fear, 38, 96, 97, 109, 120, 122, 127, 129, 130, 134, 141, 151, 165, 177
Feedback, 21, 39, 46, 58, 73, 126, 175, 181
Finkel, Donald L., v, 122, 128, 131, 168, 180, 185, 187
Five Minutes of Persuasion, 181
Five-second rule, 82, 83, 84, 85
Fong, Lisa, 103, 128, 131
Fowler, James W., 168
Free writing, 68, 92, 139
Future self, 143, 144
Gantarro Tower, 101, 103, 131
Gladness, 4, 50–52, 133, 135, 136, 138, 147, 154

INDEX

Glaspell, Susan, 24
Goals, 11, 20, 43, 45, 52, 66, 67, 74, 106, 125, 142, 172, 177
Goals, student, 125
Goldberg, Natalie, 92, 123, 131
Goodbye, retirement, 180
Goodwin, Doris Kearns, 169
Governing metaphor, 140
Grading, 118, 171
Gratitude, 180, 185
Guided imagery, 143
Haffie, Tom, xxiv, 60
Harry Potter and the Chamber of Secrets, 24
Harry Potter and the Philosopher's Stone, 24
Heads and Hearts: The Teaching and Learning Environment in Law School, 166, 189
Hellos in popular culture, 17
Hess, Gerald, 18, 128, 165, 166, 189
Home, 23, 53, 56, 65, 66, 99, 137, 138, 140, 145, 148, 158, 169, 177–179, 183
Howell, William S., 54, 60
Humor, 9, 19, 31, 84, 153, 166
Hunger, of world, 136–138
Identity, 4, 7, 23, 66, 97, 99, 133, 136, 138, 139, 164
Inauthenticity, 163
Individual Reflection Event, 39
Institute for Law School Teaching, 44, 48, 92

Institute for Law Teaching and Learning, 128
Institute for the Advancement of Teaching in Higher Education, xxii
Integrated life, 146, 164
Internal processes, 29, 89, 147, 149, 150, 154, 169
Interviewing, 9, 78, 87
Introductions, 9, 10, 12, 14, 15, 175
Invitations (to new paths), 150
Ishiguro, Kazuo, 162, 169
Job description, compose, 141, 142
Journaling, 29, 32, 41, 50, 56, 58, 68, 92, 154
Joy, 136, 138, 140
Kabat-Zinn, Jon, 34, 53, 60
Kingston, Ontario, 191
Kitchen Table Wisdom: Stories that Heal, 83
Laptops, 12, 13, 18, 34–37, 57, 183
Lawyers as Counselors: A Client-Centered Approach, 93
Learning in Groups: New Directions for Teaching and Learning, 131, 168
Learning space, 15
Leavenworth, Washington, 92, 139, 169
Legal Imagination (writing course), 180
Legal Studies Forum 27, 131
Legal writing, 156, 180
Lend-lease act, 149

Letter to self, 180
Levels of competence, 54
Life in school, 24, 30, 129,
  131, 168, 178, 187, 190
Line-up, 79, 89
Listening, 5, 21, 31, 37, 53,
  59, 63–93, 104, 127, 140,
  142, 150, 166, 185
Listening, active listening, 87,
  88
Listening, collecting data, 74
Listening, critical, 5, 63, 64,
  71, 75, 80, 87, 166
Listening, listening gap, 76
Listening, mindful, 53, 91
Listening, peaceful, 142
Lockhart, Gilderoy, 21–23
Louden, Jenifer, 60
*Love's Executioner & Other
  Tales of Psychotherapy*, 131
Mah, Stephanie, 100, 131
McGonagall, Minerva, 6, 7, 22
McGraw-Hill Ryerson, xxii,
  xxiii
Meditation, 32, 53, 56, 143,
  144, 191
Meditative process, 38, 150
Metaphor, governing, 140
Methodological belief, 70, 71,
  85
Methodological doubt, 70, 71,
  79
Micro-signals, 7
Mindfulness, characteristics
  of, 53
Mini-retreat, 28, 42
Monk, G. Stephen, 131, 168
Monk, Stephen G., 131, 168

Muller, Wayne, 60
Music, 4, 17, 18, 20, 40, 115,
  136, 182
Narcissa & Other Fables, 92,
  131
*No Ordinary Time: Franklin
  and Eleanor Roosevelt: The
  Home Front In World War
  II*, 169
Non-judgment, 31, 33, 34,
  38, 43, 53, 55, 87, 123, 149
Non-mindfulness, 25, 26
O'Reilley, Mary Rose, 24, 41,
  63, 80, 86, 92, 95, 122,
  125, 131, 141, 146, 161,
  168, 190
Obituary (writing exercise),
  138, 139
Objectivism, 166
Old School, 105, 109, 163
Omega Institute for Holistic
  Studies, 17
Overall, Christine, 121, 131,
  190
Palmer, Parker J., 24, 168, 169
Parallel universe thinking, 33,
  88, 123
Pearlman, Laurie Anne, 143,
  168
Performing message, 66
Permission, 26, 44, 57, 60,
  131, 136, 142, 169, 185
Peters, Jean Koh, 19, 41, 60,
  93, 191
Postcards, 178–180
Pratt, Katherine, 169
Presence, in teaching, 92, 141
Preskill, Stephen, 16, 21, 189

Prestige, 110, 145
Price, Susan C., 93
Prism (journal), 151
Processes we can trust, 29, 147
Processes, daily, 29, 147, 150
Processes, external, 89, 148, 153, 169
Processes, internal, 29, 89, 147, 149, 150, 154, 169
Radical Presence: Teaching as Contemplative Practice, 24, 92, 141, 168, 190
Reading aloud, 14, 116, 179
Rechtschaffen, Stephan, 17, 24, 56, 60
Reflection, 25–61, 180
Reflection, elements of, 28, 29, 31
Reflection, five-point scale, 54
Reflection, habit of, 52, 53
Reflection, individual reflection event, 39
Reflection, individual session of reflection, 39
Reflection, mindful, 52, 55
Reflection, practice of, 52
Reflection, starting focal point, 31, 32
Relief, 23, 83, 180, 182
Remen, Rachel Naomi, 83
Representing Children in Child Protective Proceedings: Ethical and Practical Dimensions, 60, 93
Representing children, 60, 93, 137, 174, 187, 191
Representing parents, 137

Representing refugees, 137, 191
Rest, 34, 60, 66, 96, 106, 108, 111, 118, 121, 149, 164
Retirement, 180
Retreat, first, 8
Retreat, second, 177
Retreat, third, xxiii
Ribbon exercise, 3, 8, 177
Rituals, 20, 29, 56
Roosevelt, Franklin Delano, 148
Routine, daily, 31, 150, 183
Rowling, J.K., 7, 24
Rules for Writing Practice, 123
Saakvitne, Karen, 143, 168
Sabbath, 27, 60
Sacred space,
Sellers, Scott, 169
September 11, 147
Serendipity, 150
Set an intention, 42
Shenker, Israel, 169
Shields, Carol, 151, 152
Shopping periods, 18
Silent witness, 178–180
Skywalker, Luke, 138
Solitude, 29, 38, 50, 149, 154
Space, for learning, 15
Sparrow, Sophie, 60, 139
Spirituality, 42, 138
Star Trek (series), 61
Star Trek: The Next Generation (series), 61
Star Wars, 138
Stories, 24, 46, 75, 83, 98, 131, 134, 137, 151, 163, 189

Stress, 34, 60
Students' names, 18
Sui Generis, 103–108, 131
Teacher-student relationship,
    7, 18, 21, 23, 165, 166,
    172, 173, 178
Teaching who we are, 23
*Teaching With Your Mouth
    Shut*, 187, 189
Technology, in classroom, 18
*The Alchemy of Race and
    Rights: Diary of a Law
    Professor*, 169, 180
*The Courage to Teach:
    Exploring the Inner Land-
    scape of a Teacher's Life*, 24,
    168, 190
The Death of the Profane, 156,
    169
The Empathic Communicator,
    54, 60
The Emperor of Ocean Park,
    92, 131
*The Five Habits for Cross-
    Cultural Lawyering*, 60
The Jade Peony, 152
The Peaceable Classroom, 24,
    131, 168, 190
The Remains of the Day, 162,
    169
The Vocation of a Teacher,
    131, 134, 155, 168, 189
The Women's Retreat Book, 60
The Writing Life, 169
Thing of Beauty, 10, 11, 20,
    123, 180–182
Timeshifting, 17, 24, 56, 60

*Timeshifting: Creating More
    Time to Enjoy Your Life*, 24,
    60
Tompkins, Jane, 24, 95, 129,
    131, 136, 168, 178, 187, 190
*Transforming the Pain:
    Workbook on Vicarious
    Traumatization*, 168
True self, 136, 163
Vacation, 140
Vocation, 4, 27, 31, 55, 116,
    131, 133–169, 189
Voice, 14, 82, 114, 129, 140,
    142, 146, 155, 160–162,
    185, 186
Voice, in writing, 162
Vulnerability, 165
Watterson, Bill, 18, 24
Weisberg, Mark, 41, 74, 120,
    168, 169, 186, 190, 191
What Is English, 24
White space, 4
White, E.B., 169
*Wild Mind: Living the Writer's
    Life*, 131
Williams, Patricia, 156, 160,
    162, 169, 190
*Wishful Thinking: The Seeker's
    ABCs*, 168
Wolff, Tobias, 163
Work/life balance, 65
Writing, 3, 6, 9, 25, 29–31,
    35, 42, 45–50, 52, 56, 57,
    64, 68, 75, 77, 80, 92, 99,
    106, 123, 124, 135, 137,
    139, 144, 150–156,
    160–162, 164–166, 169,
    180, 182, 183, 185, 191

Writing, legal, 156, 180
Writing, voice in, 162
Yalom, Irvin D., 131